Truth IS

Truth IS

An Experience To Help Reveal Your Truth

"TRUTH that you need to know that should've been taught to you, but could only be learned through experience"

Written by Tonya R

Health, Wealth & Lifestyle Lessons for modern day women (...and men)

Copyright © 2016 Tonya R
All rights reserved.

ISBN-13: 9780692764978
ISBN-10: 0692764976

Acknowledgements

BEFORE I EVEN think about giving thanks to any human I have to give my almighty God all the praises. Because I know that without his glory and mercy I would not be. Because of God's grace and my faith in Jesus I'm able to share my truths as I know they relate to each of you in some form.

Thank you readers for trusting baby truth enough to purchase my book. Thank you to my hubby Terrell, my kids Lakeah and TJ for putting up with my madness. Thank you to my bestie Monique for Always being there. Thank you to my friend Nisha for inspiring me to complete this book and many other things.

Thank you to my sisters/friends/associates Nikki, Dee Dee, Sandra, Kim, Dallas, Kizzie, Ronnique, Tam, Ruth, Sheena, Wendy, Adrienne, Scotti, Heather, Bridgette for listening to my truths. Thank you to my cousin Viva for always being there. Thank you to my Mother Karla, mother in law Terry for both being Taurus (bull headed) with their truth it helped mold me into the woman I am. Thank you to my aunt Linda for being like the sister I've always wanted. Last but not least, thank you to all my wonderful social media friends, followers, clients, and partnerships that I've made because without y'all this wouldn't be possible.

Thank you all who have supported me from day one. I love y'all and thank you for loving me. If I forgot anyone please change it to my head and not my heart!

Xoxo

Dear Reader,

My dream for this book of my TRUTHS is to inspire you to elevate your life in all aspects by changing your mindset to be kindhearted in a coldhearted world.

Love, Tonya

"My message is simple -- KNOW THYSELF! My delivery is profound. My inspiration is life changing and transforming. I've used my≈life as an example of how to overcome emptiness, loneliness, depression, lack of confidence, lack of self-love, and trying to please others. To deliver a powerful message of redemption, self-love, and purpose through my TRUTHS. As an Aries, I can be very blunt. My words can sometimes cut like a knife and can sometimes be medicine for an aching soul. My purpose is to inform women that the time is NOW to take charge of their lives by accepting and≈learning how to accentuate responsibility and accountability for their own happiness. "

Mom, Muse, Mogul

My Truth

TRUTH IS... ONE day I woke up and realized that I wasn't living, but I was merely existing. I realized that I was almost thirty-five years old and I had yet to live my life. I was 18 years old when I found a love for real estate. Right after high school, I went straight and enrolled in school to get my real estate license. My aunt had a boyfriend who was a real estate broker and he would brag about how much his commission checks were just from one sale! It was more than what some people make in 6 months on a job. I always had big dreams and pictured myself living in a big mansion behind the gates, with a driver to chauffer me around. I loved the finer things, which happened to be expensive, so of course it was evident that I would pursue a career in real estate. Additionally, the sensation I would get from selling a home to someone and then walking them through the home was exciting and only fed my hunger. College was definitely out of the picture after I sold my first house and received that FAT ASS commission check. I was like "DAMNNNNNNN!" That's when my life as an entrepreneur began! I was 23 when I bought my first house and I had 6 figures in the bank saved with more cash flowing in.

I had my own real estate company, mortgage company, and processing company. I bought houses, sold them and rented them out to tenants. I sailed high in the real estate market and helped a lot of people in the process. I've been with only one man, whom I married at age 24. Together we made two wonderful children, traveled, shopped, and made a lot of money. I always drove foreign cars and enjoyed the finer things. My hair stayed done and outfits were always on point. But guess what... my car note, my mortgage, my cell phone bill, and every bill was always late getting paid. Although I had the money to pay it, I just didn't pay until last minute. My husband and I were arguing every day and every night. He was cheating and disrespecting me. He was mentally abusive, a liar and so much more. I just felt so empty, insecure, and powerless every day. Something was telling me that I had to make some changes before I became a dead woman walking I had everything that most women would want but something was still missing. I wasn't fulfilled on the inside. In my head I had it going on, but I was still missing something. I had no idea what was missing or what I was feeling. I only knew that I had to make a change or I would just be like a mummy -- wrapped in bondage, trapped, and stuck! I wanted to pursue my dreams and make a difference but I wasn't sure what was for me.

Up until that point, I thought I was doing it all right. Shit, was I wrong! At that very moment I made a complete mindset shift. Instead of running into a wall with my issues, I faced them head on! I did so by finding a mirror, staring into that mirror for hours, and crying my heart out as I started to deal with the INTERNAL issues that blocked my OUTTER blessings… my INNER ME. It spoke back to me and I started to do a "MINDSET MAKEOVER" I needed to know who Tonya was, what Tonya wanted, and then my journey to self-love began. In this book, I'll share with you some very important stories on how I grew in love with myself, with my TRUTH, and how you can too!

"SELF LOVE IS THE BEST LOVE"

inTRUTHduction

(introduction)

MY FIRST BOOK was an urban fiction novel – a totally different genre and mindset at that time back in 2009. I started with my love for street stories like your coldest Winter ever. I loved them so much that I decided to write about the hood life, that I once lived, but on a different level… with a different taste of creativity. I didn't know where it would land me but I knew that my novel titled "Grimey Enough" would just open the doors for me to do what I truly love; to upgrade, enhance, and transform as many lives as I can with my TRUTHS. My hope is that someone can use them as a stepping stone to a higher thought process and begin to elevate to their most desired and deserving lifestyle.

I knew that once I began to inspire others with my truths that it wouldn't be long before urban fiction would be behind me and I'll be doing everything in my power to change as many lives as I can for the better with my truths. The good, the bad, and the pit bull dog ass ugly. This is not your typical advice guide. The ask-a-question-and-I'll- answer-it type of book. I'd rather tell you my truths by putting them into short stories, blunt facts, affirmations, quotes, and truth because that's how I like to learn. I like to get a visual, an idea, an actual scenario to the story. So I'll leave it up to you the readers to take what you need and want from this book and apply it …or just read and enjoy!

I get hundreds of emails from men and women wanting advice or just wanting to vent to me about their lives issues in hopes that I can help. I realized that if I was going to be the one to help people sort thru their lives, I didn't want to be one of those internet gurus who would only post status updates all day on Facebook, reply through comments, direct messages, or twitter retweets, etc. To do that would put me on the same level as other so called "coaches, mentors, etc). So I decided to achieve a goal I've had to become a certified life coach and take my TRUTHS of life and put them in black and white so they can make sense to you. If it was done, I did it. ...and I learned from it.

So in this book I've compiled most of my TRUTHS from real life situations that all people can relate to, are going through, or have been through. Wives, husbands, single women, single men, single parents, can all benefit and elevate their lives from my TRUTHS. I basically laid out the solution to most problems to help you jumpstart or restart your life. Whatever you're going through, trust and believe someone is going through too or have been through at one point in their life. But let me keep it real and please don't get it twisted, TRUTH IS is not a feed-your-ego, pamper-your-ass, pet-your-flesh, sugarcoat, tell-you-something to-make-you-feel-good type of book. I'm not your traditional smile-all-day, life is-all-sprinkles-and-glitter, The-sun-always-shines type of life coach either. I deliver the hardcore truth rather you're ready for it or not. Truth is not always wanted but it is necessary and it doesn't always hurt. Truth heals.

THIS IS THE ONE! READY TO GET YOUR LIFE TOGETHER? Well look no further! You've got the book right here!

"This is a real raw guide with a list of my truths for this generation of women who are dedicated to themselves, the women who want more out of life, the women who knows that there is no sky limit, the women who dreams are so big that they scare the shit out of them, the women that are move makers and game changers. Get ready to change your mindset and be motivated as I show you how to create a powerful, positive, mindset and help design your life on your own terms. There is some truth inside this book for everyone, in every situation. By the time you finish this experience you will begin living in your truth and that's when absolutely no one can use your truths against you!

TRUTH IS is not meant to be read in one sitting; it's designed to encourage you with proven insight, tools, tricks, and lessons to work on at your own pace. Giving yourself time to let it ALLLLLLL sink in. There's random life lessons, reference lists, recipes, activities, and plenty of resources to help take you one step closer to becoming the woman, the GODDESS, the QUEEN, that God created you to be. Whether you believe it applies to your life or not, be open minded and complete the book and just watch how you will get an opportunity to apply your new knowledge.

Here's some steps that will help make this guide work for you:

1. All my affirmations should be spoken aloud and really let is resonate in your spirit
2. Go through the lessons and the notes and really take the time to complete them with a clear mind.
3. Be patient. Nothing happens overnight – especially a new you.
4. Take what is useful and apply it to your life and let go of what is useless.
5. As you read takes notes of your "AHA" moments. Underline, highlight, and mark this book up. Make the best use of it.

Remember: every small change makes a difference and you should celebrate every single accomplishment as you use these lessons in your life. The more you celebrate the more you will have to celebrate.

"THE TRUTH HURTS, BUT MY TRUTH HEALS"

— TONYA RUSH

Truth IS

TRUTH IS… this book is dedicated to those who seek to be better than they were yesterday.

TRUTH IS… this book is dedicated to the ones who have been counted out. NOW, I'm counting you in!

TRUTH IS… this book is dedicated to the ones who understand that life is crazy sometimes.

TRUTH IS… this book is dedicated to the ones who thinks they have no worth.

TRUTH IS… this book is dedicated to those who need to see a different point of view.

TRUTH IS… this book is dedicated to those who want to make a change in their lifestyle (love, finances, spiritual journey, mindset, self-love and physically).

TRUTH IS… this book is dedicated to the ones who lost their way and need guidance on another level.

TRUTH IS… this book is dedicated to those who are ready to elevate their lifestyle.

"CHANGE YOUR MINDSET, CHANGE YOUR LIFE"

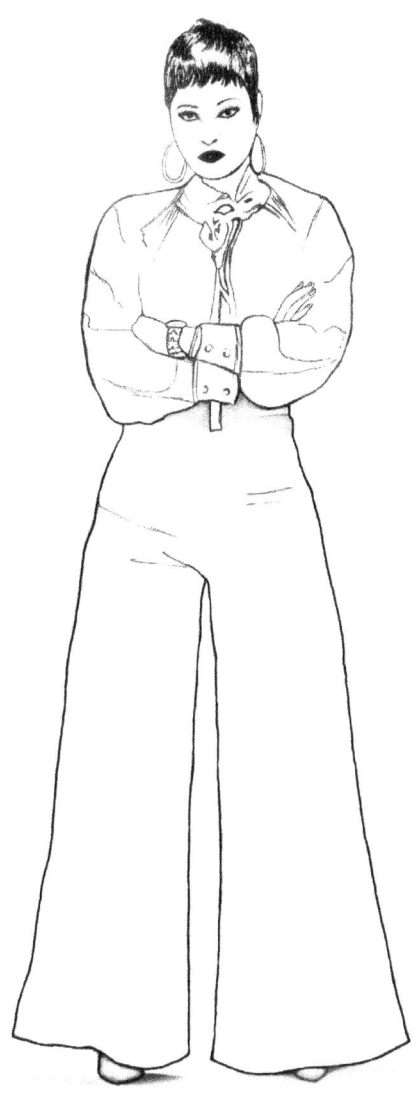

My Truths

AFFIRMATIONS
BUSINESS
LOVE
QUOTES
DOMESTIC
MINDSET
A MAN'S POINT OF VIEW

Say "I Do" To Yourself

Truth IS

IT WAS THE beginning of the summer, and we all know there are parties going on everywhere and plenty of nightlife activities brewing. So it was definitely a must to get a pedicure and manicure because if your feet weren't on point, you were considered basic. I decided to treat myself to a mani-pedi.

I was sitting in one of those pedicure booths getting a pedicure as the massager was massaging my back as my nail tech hooked me up for the night. Sitting right next to me was a very well groomed, stylish, young woman. It was clear to me that she took very good care of herself.

She sat there with her Gucci bag, Gucci shades, and Gucci belt. All of which caught my eye because of my love for nice things. She was dressed to a T with nothing much on but jeans and a tank-top. Her 3 David Yurman bracelets made a soothing sound as she moved her arm. Her make-up was as flawless and beat as the women getting ready for the Grammys. I swear in my eyes she seemed to really have her shit in order. As I continued to have a conversation with my nail tech discussing clothes and shoes she must've overheard. We made eye contact very briefly. I smiled at her, while she didn't smile back at me. Being a people person, I sparked a conversation with the young lady because I was curious as to what it was that she did to 'look like money'.

Some would say I'm a bit nosey but I say inquisitive.

So I asked her what did she do for a living, what area she lived in, who her man was, etc. because she was laced in MONEY. But from what I can tell, as she answered my questions, she seemed kind of off. Her energy wasn't genuine happiness, her voice sounded like a hall of emptiness – just my opinion. She went on and on proceeding to tell me about how much she shops, and how she never has time for herself, how much she hated her job, how empty her bank account is, and how she got to get away sometimes to go get some alone time to feel better about life because her life would be chaotic without it. She was really being transparent with me.

Then she proudly said, "Girl yes I have to treat myself, because self-love is the key"

At that very moment, I realized that the emptiness I heard in her voice and sadness on her face was a cry for help, a silent cry, but no one could help but herself. No one knows the answer but YOU. Self-love is all women say it is, "self-love is the best love" and "I love me". Blah, blah blah. We've allowed that message to become a taint for the unauthentic.

TRUTH IS… just because you're going to the nail shop, going to Chicago and Miami to shop, keeping your hair fly and nails on point, does not mean that you love yourself. That's merely what we call pampering yourself. To be honest, pampering yourself while your bank account is always empty is not self-love honey. So many women got this self-love thing twisted. Making yourself look good on the outside is never equal to feeling good about yourself on the inside.

TRUTH IS… you're just giving the money that you complained about not having to the mall, your hairstylist, and nail techs on a regular basis. To be appealing to folks that don't even matter. Your dressed, footed, and booted from top to bottom, and your hair is on point but your spirit is begging for just a little attention.

Self-love is the most misunderstood and inappropriately used phrase because it's from the inside and that's something you have to attend to. Self-love means making YOU priority number one. Self-love means being a little bit selfish for your own wellbeing. Self-love means giving your spirit, your mind, your inside body and heart what they need, when they need it at the time they need it. It means slowing down with life's emotional roller coaster and giving your spirit a chance to catch up with your body. Self-love is appreciating your physical body for giving you what its allowed you to do and gratefully appreciating your mind for the decisions it allowed you to make. It means analyzing your values, morals and beliefs, and not compromising your worth to please to someone else and downgrading your expectations and standards MERELY to satisfy someone else's expectations. Self-love is about loving yourself in the same way that you want someone else to love you. Its making the time to do what your man, your friends, your children, and your family do for you. Self-love is speaking to yourself with respect, listening to yourself, trusting your inner voice (intuition) and treating yourself like the Queen that you were born to be.

TRUTH IS… 75 percent of women spend a majority of their lives taking care of other people. People such as your children, your man, your husband, your boss, your friends, your bills, and your homes. More than half of the time, everyone is being nurtured and loved way before we are nurturing and loving ourselves. Its un-empowering when you let everyone and everything feed from your half full cup of life. But then you're always wondering why you're so tired, why you're always broke, why you're gaining weight that's making you feel less confident, why you keep headaches, why you get so annoyed by others so easily, why your sex life is boring as watching water boil, and why you can't experience the feeling of deep passionate love in your life.

Before you can honestly say that you have self-love and that you are living in your self-love truths, you have to know what those two words "self" and "love" mean to you.

Who are YOU and how do YOU need to be loved? What does love mean to you? I know that it wakes some serious soul searching and life experiences to truly understand what love is. It takes you listening to your heart, mind body and soul and understanding exactly what you need to nurture for growth. It takes you being completely honest with yourself, your flaws and all. It takes forgiving yourself for not loving yourself right. Commit to loving YOU, you deserve it.

HERES A FEW WAYS THAT I PRACTICE SELF LOVE, AND HOPEFULLY YOU CAN PRATICE THEM AS WELL SO THAT YOU TOO, WILL LOVE YOURSELF.

1. *Talk to yourself with respect and generosity. We try to speak to others with respect but we are soo hard on ourselves. We say the meanest, most discouraging, hurtful things, like "I'm fat"," I'm broke", "I can't do this"," It's just not for me". INSTEAD of saying "I'm fat" say "I really need to go to the gym and get my body looking like a four season body". INSTEAD of saying "I'm Broke" say "I might not have what I need right now money-wise, but I will be wealthy soon".*

   Tell yourself "I LOVE YOU", every time you look in the mirror or walk pass one.

   You don't have to say it out loud each time but make sure you do sometimes. Speak to yourself with love and compassion. Tell yourself how proud of you that you are. Tell yourself that you can be and do whatever you want. Being able to spill life into yourself is a very challenging thing to possess but the easiest thing to do. If you don't who else will?

2. Be a little SELFISH. *If you've ever been on an airplane and upon take off the attendants say in case of an emergency, please put your oxygen mask on first. Have you thought about what would happen to other people had you not put yours on first? You definitely wouldn't be able to help anyone because you have to help yourself before you can help others. How can I help you if I haven't been through your situation or if I'm broken myself? There's no way I can give you what you need if my needs aren't met by ME. For example, saying NO is so hard for so many people. You have to start telling people who ask to borrow money NO especially when you know you have bills due. Who's going to pay your bills for you now that you've loaned out money that you didn't really have.*

   Another example is NOT answering the phone when your girl calls at 3AM crying to you about that SAME nothing ass boyfriend of hers singing the same old song, not because you don't care, but because you are tired and need some rest. That's when being selfish is for you, and not so much of a bad thing. Remember your cup has to be full before you can attempt to help fill someone else's cup!

3. READ, READ, READ! *You could never know too much. The more you know the more you grow. Knowledge is power when applied correctly.*

There's so much we don't know and could easily know just by reading. Do something different. Learn another way. Get off of the trolley of life, doing the same things over and over expecting a different result. Enhance your skills and elevate your mindset so that you can get more out of life.

"YOU are your own guru. YOU are your own soul mate. YOU are powerful. Take the reins and drive your carriage home to love."

— Amy Leigh Mercree

Maya Angelou's Best Poem Ever

A WOMAN SHOULD HAVE... Enough money within her control to move out...And rent a place of her own even if she never wants to or needs to...

A WOMAN SHOULD HAVE... Something perfect to wear if the employer or date of her dreams wants to See Her in an hour...

A WOMAN SHOULD HAVE... A youth she's content to leave behind....

A WOMAN SHOULD HAVE... A past juicy enough that she's looking forward to retelling it in her Old Age....

A WOMAN SHOULD HAVE... A set of screwdrivers, a cordless drill, and a black lace bra...

A WOMAN SHOULD HAVE... One friend who always makes her laugh... And one Who lets her cry...

A WOMAN SHOULD HAVE... A good piece of furniture not previously owned by anyone else in her Family...

A WOMAN SHOULD HAVE.... Eight matching plates, wine glasses with stems, and a recipe for a meal that will make her guests feel Honored...

A WOMAN SHOULD HAVE... A feeling of control over her destiny...

EVERY WOMAN SHOULD KNOW... How to fall in love without losing herself.

EVERY WOMAN SHOULD KNOW... How to quit a job, break up with a lover, and confront a friend without ruining the friendship.

EVERY WOMAN SHOULD KNOW... When to try harder...And when to walk away.

EVERY WOMAN SHOULD KNOW... That she can't change the length of her calves, the width of her hips, or the nature of her parents.

EVERY WOMAN SHOULD KNOW... That her childhood may not have been perfect... but it's over

EVERY WOMAN SHOULD KNOW... What she would and wouldn't do for love or more.

EVERY WOMAN SHOULD KNOW... How to live alone, even if she doesn't like it.

EVERY WOMAN SHOULD KNOW... Whom she can trust, whom she can't, and why she shouldn't take it personally.

EVERY WOMAN SHOULD KNOW... Where to go. Be it to her best friend's kitchen table or a charming inn in the woods when her soul needs soothing.

EVERY WOMAN SHOULD KNOW... What she can and can't accomplish in a day, a month, and a year.

Tonya R

What does this poem mean to me: _____

If you don't know who Maya is I suggest you Google Maya Angelou to learn more about her!

Humble yourself or God will do it for you

It was 2006 and the real estate market was hot. It was a time when you can literally become a millionaire over a few short months. If you were in this industry you were either an agent, an investor, mortgage loan officer or hard money lender. It was a time when obtaining property was easier than obtaining a vehicle. I had the real estate market on lock. I was a real estate agent, investor, and owned my own mortgage company. Friends at the title company and hard money lenders in my front and back pockets. I had clients all over Missouri who was bringing me their deals. I was making a minimum of 25K a month and owned several rental properties. I was cashing and depositing checks left and right. Buying cars and more property. You couldn't tell me anything!

During that time, I knew that my head blew up. I was young and wealthy and in my eyes I was the shit so yes the arrogance kicked in. Nose up and only dealing with certain people. Only with the people who were living like me, driving cars like mine or people who could put money in my pocket. It was all about the dollars for me. But that could and would only last so long.

Later in 2009, the real estate market started to decline. People were losing their homes because they couldn't make the payments. I started losing my rental properties and my hard money lenders stopped giving me money. My clients declined as well because they were losing their properties also. I was lost. I didn't know what to do. Real estate was all that I knew. I had been in the industry since the age of 18. So slowly my funds that I saved were being spent to pay this and that because I had so much material debt, and when there's no money coming in but money going out that money goes a lot faster. I lost my mortgage company because I couldn't pay the rent for my office space anymore. I couldn't keep the lights on. I was borrowing money from all my friends and family. People would hate to see me coming because they thought I was begging. It was a very terrible time especially for someone who was used to always having it all. I was soon months behind on my mortgage at home. Lights off at home. Gas off. I quickly realized, that Karma is something. I took a long hard look at my life at that point and where it went wrong then I realized it was because God wasn't in my business and I had to humble myself.

TRUTH IS...
Often times we hear certain adages or proverbs such as, "cast all your cares on the Lord because He cares for you..." and we stop there and apply that to our lives and our situations. That is absolutely ok. But what I find so phenomenal is that when I study my Bible, that one adage is most times linked to some other criteria or lessons that we must adhere to in order to reap the greatest return or harvest on our prayers. Here Peter reminds us to be humble! Humble ourselves to each other and to God. We are reminded that pride will be our undoing and we will be resisted by God, but with humility grace is freely given. Humility comes before exaltation! And it all comes in due time!

We need not worry about the time or the how or the this or the that. We must have faith and turn it over to God. We are all children of God and just like a young child, we try and do life on our own. But as always is the case something comes up that just beats us down or tries us or tempts us to the point we revert to a small child humbly submitting to our parent acknowledging we don't/can't do it and with grace and with love, our parent takes over. Keep a clear mind! A noisy, cloudy mind is unstable.

Stay positive in your thoughts! Give no opportunities for doubt or negativity to creep in.

TRUTH IS...
After a while, you don't care what people say. After a while, you don't hang with the friends you used to hang-out with. After a while, you don't care if the besties stay or not. After a while, you get tired of all the drama in your life. After a while, you're not the same person you used to be. After a while, you

just want the better things in life & you going to do whatever it takes to get your life in order the way you want it! And lastly, after a short while.

TRUTH IS…
As long as you are focused on people, you will not be able to see where God is taking you. Take the limits off!! Keep your eyes on the prize!

TRUTH IS…
Don't say a word just sit back and watch. When something is right no need to show off but simply thank God. He knows how to elevate you and not the other way around. Less is more! Hear me there is always someone plotting for your demise but it will not happen. Always pray for the best for others but watch those pretenders. Feed them with a long handle spoon as my grandmother would say!

TRUTH IS….
When you lie you never have rest! Why? Because it's not the truth!

My mom always told me what's done in the dark will come to the light. Sit back folk and watch God bring all things against you to a head. Popcorn time!

TRUTH IS…
I promise you I have drunk more water with a straw than without it! Without thinking all the water is gone. If you want to increase your water intake drink with a straw!

TRUTH IS…
Looking from outside trying to judge a situation will leave you with outer court information. If you want to know ask and stop assuming. Second hand information is simply venom waiting on the right ear to subtly go in for the kill. Watch who brings you a bone.

TRUTH IS….
You cannot please everybody. So stop trying! Now doesn't that truth feel good?

TRUTH IS...
The struggle is not real. It is real to you, maybe. It doesn't take material gains to be happy. You can make the decision to appreciate the life you have and make the best of it. Stop looking at what someone else has believing that their HAPPY will be our HAPPY or should be your HAPPY. Everything isn't always what it seems. A lot of people live a façade meaning, for show simply to please the outside eyes.

What's your HAPPY?

_____
_____
_____
_____
_____
_____
_____
_____
_____
_____
_____
_____
_____
_____
_____
_____
_____
_____
_____
_____
_____
_____
_____
_____

TRUTH IS…

Some issues are passed down from generation to generation! You have the power to tell that issue that it ends with you.

Have you ever heard the term, "the apple doesn't fall far from the tree" or "she gets it from her momma?" Well in most cases that's true because that's what you're being taught. From family to family. You were taught it that way so you taught your kids and so on. What are you going to do differently?

Starting today, I am going to
_____
_____
_____
_____
_____
_____
_____
_____
_____
_____
_____
_____
_____
_____
_____
_____
_____
_____
_____
_____
_____

Treat Your Man like a Dog

TRUTH IS.....
THE BIGGEST FACTOR in determining the quality of our relationship is the way we view other people, particularly our partner. There are many books, seminars and couples retreats that are designed to help you improve your relationship. But is there something we can possibly learn from treating our partner the way we treat our dog?

This advice might sound a little unusual, but just go with me for a second.

We accept our dog unconditionally, because we know they're a dog. We don't expect them to be what they're not, because they're completely authentic. Acceptance is the greatest gift you can give to a person (or a dog) because it's the greatest sign of respect. Respect builds trust and without trust there is no relationship.

Here are 5 lessons we can learn from our furry friends:

1. Accept your partner just as he or she is.
We accept our pets just as they are, we don't expect them to be anything else. If our dog does something we don't like, we may get upset and reprimand them, but we almost immediately forgive them. We think, "well, after all they're just a dog" or "they're just being natural."

Dogs don't try to be something that they're not. They are completely authentic. They react to their environment and their natural instincts. Because we know this, we accept them.

If we can learn to accept our partner just as they are, our relationships will transform miraculously. Accepting your partner completely is the biggest sign of respect you can give them. It means you love and respect them enough to know they're making their decisions based on what they know is right.

That doesn't mean you can't offer them support and guidance, but you don't find them guilty for not being who you think they should be. After all, they're not you; they are themselves

2. People, like dogs, react better to reward than punishment.
When we pick out all the things we don't like about our dog, we're focusing only on the negative. When we constantly punish them for being who they are, we're telling them it's not okay to be who they are. This only creates feelings of guilt and resentment.

It works the same way with our partners. When we focus on all the negative things about them, we're sending them a subliminal message: we don't think it's okay for them to be who they are. People often defend themselves by saying something like "I only try to help them because I care" or "I just love them so much that I want to make them better." But this type of behavior simply leads a person to feel like they're constantly being rejected. They're never good enough.

If we instead focus on the positive attributes of the other person, we send them a message of acceptance. When a person knows that we respect them enough to accept them as they are, they'll also be more likely to take our criticism and guidance. People need to know that you see their strengths first, before their flaws.

3. Love comes from within first, with out second.
Our dogs may seek our approval, love and acceptance, but they don't rely on it. They have their own sense of joy, playfulness and love that comes from within. They enjoy our company and love, but their sense of self doesn't come from it.

When our sense of self comes from our partner, we leave ourselves vulnerable to the ups and downs of the relationship. When our partner acts in a loving way, we feel good. But when our partner is unloving, we feel down. This is because our source of love is rooted with out, not within.

When we find love from within ourselves first, we have a much greater capacity to give it. We're not relying on our partner to give it to us. This also makes it much easier to love our partner when they are not so loving towards us.

4. Be compassionate, but don't be a doormat.
Often people have a hard time drawing the line between when to show compassion and when to show tough love. I think this conflict is due to a misunderstanding. Sometimes tough love is the greatest sign of compassion.

We all know when something is not good for someone, in our own hearts. This isn't the kind of judgment that's just based on our own opinion of the right way to do things. It's more based on knowing when a habit is something that is unhealthy.

For example, say your partner is a smoker. Obviously, you know this is an unhealthy habit and could have serious and negative consequences if they don't change. Expressing your concern in this case doesn't mean you're coming down on them. It comes from a place of love and genuine concern. You may not want to criticize them, but confrontation and letting them know where you stand is necessary. This is a greater sign of love and compassion than ignoring the problem because you don't want to seem like a nag. In fact, ignoring it — whether we want to believe it or not — is really just a kind of silent approval.

Sometimes you have to give your partner tough love, just like you would your pet. You may not want to make them feel bad, but it will really benefit them in the long run.

5. Forgive and forget.
When our pet does something wrong and we lose our temper, they naturally feel ashamed, as though they let us down. They might resent us for a while, because in their mind they didn't know any better. But they forgive much more quickly then we humans tend to.

We humans, on the other hand, have a powerful memory and tend to take things personally. We have a feeling of personal importance; that whatever "they" did it must be about me. But usually, it wasn't about you at all. It was about them. Whatever someone does to hurt you, it really has nothing to do with you. It was their beliefs, opinions and feelings that caused them to react the way they did. It's easy to see this when you know that the more emotional security and self-esteem you have, the less likely you are to take offense to others wrongs. On the other hand, the more emotional baggage you carry around, the more likely you'll take offense to others actions. In psychology, this is what we call projection.

This whole way of thinking stems from personal importance and trying to live up to an image of perfection that we have in our minds. We think that we should be a certain way, but we know we aren't. So we find ourselves guilty[7] and punish ourselves. We play the game of the judge and the victim constantly in our minds. Because we do this so much with ourselves, we naturally[7] do this with others. We don't know any better.

Dogs on the other hand are completely authentic. They know that they are a dog and they accept it. They don't try to be something they're not and they don't expect you to be something you're not. That's why if its so easy for your dog to forgive you when you do something wrong. If there's one thing we can learn from our canine friends, it is forgiveness.

Saddie my 24year old yorkie taught me a lot about the perfect relationship. It's based on unconditional acceptance. She loves me just the way I am, as long as I play with her and take her potty, she thinks I'm an angel. As long as she doesn't steal my food (she has a thing for croissants) or bite my foot, then we usually get along.

She doesn't have many expectations of me and I don't for her. She may get on my nerves when she wines at the foot of the stairs for what seems like hours, but I soon forgive her. I know she's just being herself and wants her daddy to wake up and play with her. And if I don't play with her, she doesn't take it personally; she just goes and does her own thing. Most likely chewing her bone or playing with spider.

A grain of salt.

This TRUTH isn't meant to be taken completely literally. Obviously there are some big differences between romantic relationships and the relationships you have with a pet. Also, a lot of people assume master/servant roles (you decide which is which, with cats it can get confusing =P), which shouldn't be applied to human or romantic relationships. Some people see their pets as their children as well as some people are abusive to their pets. These are two more examples where you shouldn't translate the your pet relationship to your relationship with your partner.

Most importantly, we should take this advice with a grain of salt and take away the lessons of forgiveness and acceptance. If we can apply this to our personal relationships, we can see there's a lot to be learned from our humble friends.

A Man's Point of View

Tonya R

By: Oliver Sparton

> "If a man is literally just chilling with you with no sense of urgency, then he thinks that your relationship is a good time, nothing more."

So I guess you're wondering how men view you, ladies. Well, there are many different layers to this question and to answer it we have to break down each layer one at a time.

In order to do this, I'm going to name each layer after a guy.

The first man is "The Scorn Man". The scorn man is a man that has been hurt since childhood. This man has either grown up around an abusive dad or been without a father and has seen his mom date her fair share of male friends. This man will see you ladies as an obstacle to cross. He will see all the things that you've been through and want to make it better because somewhere deep down inside you lies his happiness as well. This man isn't necessary a bad man but often times he meets women who are just getting out of a relationship and he ends up getting hurt even more. This man will see you as a liar and never fully open up to you. No matter how many times he cries to you there will be shades of gray areas around his life that you won't see until he has hurt you, directly or indirectly.

He will see you as someone who is better than him and for that reason alone will cling to you all the time. His reason for clinging to you will be because of his bad relationship with his mom. In a weird but freaky way, you remind him of all the things his mom really is or was going to be. This man will never believe anything you say because of his insecurities and will often show signs of an abusive person. He will always have a mole in your inner circle for information. Since this man doesn't trust you he will always find that one friend who likes him and willing to get him information on where you've been for the last 72 hours. After breaking up with you this man will never see anything he's done wrong and will use all the hurtful things you've done to get involved with someone who reminds him of you and so on. The next man is the most important layer of them all.

The next man is "The Revenge Man". This man, ladies, has been fucked over once by someone he loved and trusted and will never go back to seeing women as an equal or a woman again. He sees women as a pawn to get what he wants and nothing more. He will come to you in your darkest hour at times saying everything you want to hear and knowing exactly how you feel because he has been there. Often you have given this man the key to your heart. You ask how, well let's see. Women tend to think and speak from their heart. For example, you met this attractive guy at the club and he seems nice and after hearing you tell him your single he asks in a firm voice, "Why are you single?" From there on out you spill everything to him form how you've been hurt and gave your ex money or how you want a XYZ type of man. A few weeks later go by and he calls you and guess which costume he has on. You guessed it, the XYZ type of guy.

This guy will never true love you and knows you will try to change him, so he will give you bits and pieces of a change man to get what he wants but deep down he knows he is winning. He knows that you hate staring over so he will be nice sometimes and him the rest of the time. He sees you as also a financier to his dreams and possibly his side woman spending habits. He will keep everything he loves and knows in his phone, which in some cases is always locked. He will have plenty of reasons for it being locked but the real one is that he is pursuing his next victim and planning an escape route after he has gotten what he wants out of you mentally, sexually, and financially. This man you also see you as everyone who has ever hurt him whether it be a girlfriend, mother, or best friend. He has no interest in you other than breaking your heart and using everything you confided in him against you. It only then and only when he has a child he sees the pain that he caused his victims. After having a daughter, he will forever make it his duty to prevent her from being hurt by someone like him, giving him the ultimate thing he hate the most, KARMA. The good guys always finish last.

The next man is "The Good Man". This is the man of your dreams. This is the guy your mom would love and your dad would be proud of you dating. Unfortunately, when you do meet this man you will have already went through so much from the other types of men it will be hard to see this person for what his worth. This man will see you as a queen and someone to confide in when he as well as you have had a bad day. The good man will tell you things like your beautiful and mean it. He will tell you as a friend that if a man is literally just chilling with you with no sense of urgency, then he thinks that your relationship is a good time, nothing more.

He won't judge you but will always wonder what makes you go back to the things you tell him that you hate. Over the course of time the good man will start to lose faith in you. He will see that you are too use to getting hurt and will never want he has to offer you, which is love and affection. He will try to stay around just in case you change your mind, but eventually a close friend of yours will see him for what he is worth and take the happiness you could have had. Unlike the rest of the men you date, the good man will always be there even after he has given up on you and the relationship. He knows that your heart is in a dark place but will frown at the chance of you wanting him when all else fails with your life.

For example, in the movie Temptation we see the good guy isn't appreciated until the girl sees what she could have had after chasing what she thought was a sure and perfect thing. The good man sees everything wrong in your life and wants to help but because you've been hurt so much you lack trusting him. This in return makes him afraid to say anything to you leaving that void to be filled by someone who doesn't have your best interest at heart. But don't feel as if you've turned a good guy bad. The good guy will stay the good guy and be friends with you, in some cases just to see you get hurt and see you experience what you wanted all along; a dream of dating him and not the reality of dating him.

In the end we men have been one if not all of these men. Everyman wants to be the man that the girl he is chasing wants. It's only after finding out that some women don't know what they want we reevaluate what we need. All men want to satisfy women, its only beyond that do they see what someone truly wants from them. When it's all said and done men will view you as you much as you view yourself.

THE END

TRUTH IS...

It is a requirement in every relationship to suffer and hurt. You can't skip that. Those fights, those chances that you may break up and make up. After that you will proudly say we've been though many difficulties yet we faced it and we are still here.

I Digress

Truth IS

I BET SOMEONE is waking up dreading to go to school or work today because they feel like the outcast. I remember those days of caring about that. In elementary and middle school, I damn near faked every illness in the book to avoid going to that place. Aaaahh I digress. Lol. I did everything in my power to make friends. I became aware for the first time about my complexion and was teased for having lighter skin, they thought I was mixed calling me an "Oreo" or a "Zebra" (original little fuckers, those kids were). I was stuck drawing pictures of my home and wishing I could hop on a plane and disappear. I wanted to fit in - but I didn't. Guess what? Fitting in is overrated! Stand out. You'll be fine. You're fucking awesome.

TRUTH IS...

- The sooner you have your own cool shit going on the sooner people will notice.
- The sooner you LOVE yourself the sooner more people will also love you.
- The sooner you stop trying to be anyone else is the moment you start attracting all the other cool non-conformists.

Be confident. You got this!

"Why try to fit in when you were born to stand out"

Time Means Nothing

TRUTH IS...

OH BOY. BE very clear. Time is nice and history is cool, but if you look back at that time and history and it's completely poisonous, what's the real value in that? There are all these wonderful people in the world that you may be overlooking because of your "loyalty" to someone who doesn't value you, respect you or love you the way you need to be loved. Dude! All these beautiful souls in the world and you're giving your energy and time to a lost soul?!

Don't put yourself on the clearance rack.

Mind Games

TRUTH IS...

YOUR MIND WILL play tricks on you. It will tell you that you aren't good enough, strong enough, or smart enough... but it's up to you to stop those thoughts in their tracks before they become something ingrained in you and actually defeat you. And if you already suffer from any kind of mental instability, it's imperative to keep your balance.

And in terms of your balance, watch your close circle carefully. Be sure that they are uplifting you rather than contributing to any negative feelings you are having about yourself. Your team should be honest and loyal but always loving in delivery.

TRUTH IS...
"YOU CAN SIT WITH ME!" This has been my motto forever! Everyone is welcome. I was never at the popular table; I was at the nice girls table. And I'm still there. Join me. If someone doesn't want to sit with you, thank them. Go find the people who accept you for you.

Everything Is Not For Social Media

TRUTH IS...

IN THIS DAY of oversharing I think we forget that some memories and moments can just be for ourselves and ourselves only. I get being so excited that we want to tell the world, but understand that not everyone is happy for you. They may even wish bad things upon you because of jealousy or dissatisfaction with their own lives. I think it's gotten so crazy that people think because you don't choose to share it that it doesn't exist and that's absolutely crazy. One little app is just a small picture of most people's lives. The part they want you to see. Don't get so busy watching other people's lives that you forget to live your own. There is so much we miss when we are staring at a screen. This is why it is important to step outside of yourself for a while. Take a break. Do something to help others. Your mind can play tricks on you and have you feeling like everything is hopeless. Bills, responsibilities, deadlines, it can all seem so overwhelming. These things won't just go away with mindfulness and meditation but you will learn how to cope with them better.

Transparency Or Nothing

TRUTH IS...

AT ONE POINT years ago I was in a psych ward with a wound on my leg from stabbing myself with a pen. I was restrained and everything was taken away from me that could be a danger to me. I know what it is like to feel hopeless. There's no shame in my story. I also know what it is to feel unexplainable joy. Joy isn't attached to anything tangible, per se. It's a state of mind that can be reached when we live with an attitude of gratitude in the present and learn to be less hard on ourselves. I was and am my own worst critic. But I have learned to be more gentle with myself. You can too. Treat your mental health as seriously as you do your physical health. Reach out to someone if you feel low. I can promise you that if you hang on better days are coming.

You were brought here for a purpose. Find it!

Faultless

TRUTH IS...
BEFORE YOU RUN around trying to find fault with others and what they do, understand that:

1. You're not perfect,
2. You have faults of your own, and
3. Pointing out other people's faults will not help you bring peace to yourself. In fact, what bothers you most about someone else is usually something that you're fighting yourself about internally.

We are all spiritual beings having a human experience. What's the point in going back and forth all day pointing out what you don't like about someone when you wouldn't want it done to you? Has social media made us lose all manners? Lead us to feel entitled to speak about or know every detail about virtual strangers? Made us so worried about the next person's business that we forgot to mind our own?

Destruction

TRUTH IS...

THE MOST TOXIC, sociopathic people have mastered the ability of trying to make themselves the victim when they get caught being destructive, cheating, lying, etc. They also have learned how to flip it on you when you call them on their behavior. They love to cause havoc and then say, "why are you upset?" or "why do you make thing so hard?" or "things could just be so easy if____." If what? If we could simply ignore the fact that they lie pathologically or that they enjoy hurting people? Yes, things will be much easier when we stop *allowing* (remember nothing continues without your permission) them to cause destruction and to manipulate our hearts and minds with their deception.

Pray, chant, meditate for them and hope that they see the Light and be glad you did too. No love lost. Bottom line, you CANNOT want to help someone more than they want to help themselves! And you cannot drown yourself trying to save someone who doesn't even realize they're drowning.

Don't Be Envious, Be Inspired

TRUTH IS... ENVY.

As YOU GROW you'll experience this on so many levels. If you're in a growing stage, get prepared. Some will like you better when you're doing bad and when God starts blessing you they'll start being distant. Pay attention to these people. It's only a matter of time before your light makes them feel a bit dim. People who are really winning love to see other people win. Many who live like this are still in the crab in the barrel mentality. They won't even @ you on IG or Facebook in fear that someone else may find your platform more interesting. I challenge you to celebrate the people you know who are doing attempting to do amazing things in life.

Power Couple, For Real

TRUTH IS...

TOGETHER, WE WILL! Here are five ways to grow a successful business with your spouse.

1. Respect your spouse's suggestions and consult with them prior to making BIG business decisions.
2. Don't force your spouse to be interested in YOUR business venture. If they're not, allow them to have their own passions in life. It doesn't mean that they don't support you, they just have different interest. Let them!
3. Remember that your spouse is your partner not your assistant. Don't be too bossy.
4. Find out what your spouse is good at and let them be great in that area of the business! It's just easier that way.
5. Be sure to focus on what you love about working together vs what you dislike about it. Everyone loves feeling appreciated.

Be Fearless

TRUTH IS...
FEAR USED TO hold me back so much in life. The fear of failing, the fear of not knowing what's next, the fear of letting go of people and the fear of starting over. I now sit and think of how those thoughts were limiting my productivity in life. I've learned to do everything that I feared doing. You will unlock a new level in your life every time you do it. You become more and more fearless as well. Today I challenge you to step past those voices in your head and do something that you've feared doing for a long time. If your dreams don't scare you, they aren't big enough.

Living Or Existing

TRUTH IS...
IF YOU KNEW your expiration date, I am pretty sure you will start living. Stop procrastinating as if you have your whole life to live! Start doing everything that it is you want to do. Yo. I be living!

THE MOMENT I HAVE A THOUGHT I ACT ON IT!

That shit made me so successful! I am rich because I'm living! Small minds would think I'm talking about money!

EVERYONE SHOULD HAVE A BUCKET LIST...WHATS FIVE THINGS ON YOURS:

1. _____
2. _____
3. _____
4. _____
5. _____

TIP: Get a passport. Travel the world. They say if you ain't traveling you aint living! The world is one big book, you got to travel to get to other chapters!

Don't Take It Personally

TRUTH IS...
DON'T TAKE IT personally.

I say this because often times It will lead into disappointment, disagreements, & angriness. It could really mess up a whole situation or relationships We may support people who have or never will support us. But in business never take it personal. Expect nothing but appreciate everything and you will go far. I have supported many individuals who have never purchased a book or supported an event I've had. However, I always say to myself "Tonya, don't take it personal"

Continue to let your blessings pour in from God ♥. When God blesses you some may feel as if you owe them apart of your blessings. I've seen this happen in so many family and friend relationships. Don't you ever feel bad about telling a person no! We all have the same 24 hours. Money changes so many things even the ones around you and often times bring trouble your way from people who don't even know you. Most call it hate.

STAY PRAYED UP!
A lot of people don't talk about this part of success which cause successful people, like myself, to become very guarded. We distance ourselves from a lot of things and a lot of people. When you stand your ground you will notice so many will start to disappear. You will even cut of those you thought would be around to share the success with you. I use to cry and question God "why?" But now I get it!

If you want success be ready for everything that comes with it ♥

TIP: Understand money doesn't make you happy nor is it supposed to change those around you.

But But God

TRUTH IS...
For a very long time I didn't think God would bless me like some of the successful free spirited people I looked up to. For a very long time I thought I was going to just live paycheck to paycheck. I always knew something had to change and something was going to change because I been through so much. But I never knew when things were going to change. It was always hard for anyone to understand my struggles because I always tried to live my best. See a person who doesn't dream would have loved my life back then but the ones who dreamed that I came across have seen right through me. Mainly, it was men. See, at that time I was searching for my big break and I thought men could give me that. I was told "a baller could change my life. At the time I was just trying to get in where I fit in.

I came across so many men who have taught me so much, I learned from every bad experience I had with a man. I kept a note of everything. I found that I was looking for someone else to give me what I needed and not once did I search for God to give me what I needed. I have lost houses, had cars repossessed, had people spread lies about me, had everyone judging me and think I was a bad person just by listing to what others said.

So they didn't support my business. These people where so good some still don't like me without even knowing or meeting me! I had so many people trying to get my business shut down!! You name it, I've been through it. So no, I'm not better, I'm not famous, and I am not a Beyoncé! I am you I am so regular and went through regular stuff just like you all, but I never let it rip my faith away!

Let me tell you about GOD! Do you know how powerful that man is? He will have everyone who ever doubted you, hurt you, or let you down, look so crazy, so dumb, and so stupid! All he needs you to do is hold it together!

So pull yourself together and get through this mess! You have a world of people to prove wrong!

Keep Your Business To Yourself

TRUTH IS...

- Which one of you has that friend who just mad about everything you do?
- Always wanting to rain on your parade?
- Which one of you has that partner who jealous of your accomplishments, and want to put you down every chance he/she gets?
- Which one of you has that oh I could or could have did that ex homie who swear he or she knows your resources/connect or someone better?
- Which one of you told someone your ideas which are now being done by the very same person you told them to?

Some of us learn things the hard way but point is that we learned, I know sometimes we get very excited and want to share every damn thing, but you must understand everybody isn't with you! Some are dancing with the devil and so good at their two-step. Soon as you tell everyone, all of a sudden shit don't happen! Hold it in! Wait till the deal is done! And not only done but secure! Everyone isn't that damn happy they will use the negative energy around them to destroy your makings! KEEP QUIET! I always say "share ONLY what you could afford to"!

Invest In You, No One Else Will

TRUTH IS...
THE ONLY WAY you will succeed in like is if you invest into your life! Money makes shit happen, your time should mean everything to you don't waste not one once of it especially in business, and effort, if you don't put effort hard work into your shit who else gone care? Man you got to make these mother fuckers believe in you and your brand or whatever it is you're trying to do if you don't put effort into your shit you aren't going to love it because you don't really give a fuck about it anyway.

Don't take no for an answer ether!!! always remember anything is negotiable! And because one person told you no, doesn't get it, or doesn't believe in your shit, fuck it! Carry on they will regret it one day once shit starts popping off! And stop talking to much your friends & family don't give a fuck especially if their situation isn't right. How are you going to expect someone to love your ambition or be happy that your trying to get rich and they aren't happy with their own shit! And if you have that you're super blessed. Find a team who loves your brand! Your movement is very important so everyone that's on your team must be passionate about your brand that's the only way you'll get rich fast cause you need help!

EVERYONE HAS TO BE ON BOARD! Everyone has to be dedicated about your brand or you're going to find yourself so stressed out doing everything on your own! And the process gone be a little slow! If they knew better, they will get on board instead of trying to beat you in everything. The one that's popping is going to take the who team to victory! LEARN LIFE!

The CEO

TRUTH IS...
I AM PROUD of my roles in life and I want all my fellow bosses, CEO'S, and leaders to be proud also! By having a business, it is your duty to never take anything personally.

You cannot run a business thinking that everybody who starts with you is going to end with you. Run a business for longevity. It is your duty to teach with the hopes they will take it and learn something from it.

As a leader, you should be happy that others are inspired by you. To take on a roll as a leader you have to not only be okay with others following your path to greatness but also teaching them to create a lane of their own.

Being a CEO is tough. It is important to be spiritually connected with God because you will need it! CEO's have many hats to fill. I say spiritual for a reason, why? Because being a CEO can cause stress, drama, and envious people in your life. People may feel they can't do the same thing as you or feel they deserve the position not you! Being a CEO you have to run everything and to be able to do that you have to be sane enough to handle all the things that's thrown your way.

Fake Support

TRUTH IS...
THEY CAN'T SUPPORT you in public because OF how they speak about you in private.

> But guess what…
>
> 1.) That's none of your business
> 2.) If you want god to bless you tremendously you don't want fake supporters anyway.
> 3.) What someone says about you or feel about you changes absolutely nothing in your life.
> 4.) Stop taking everything so personal.

You busy winning you have 0 time to care about who isn't supporting you. Take me for an example! Have I lost anything? Absolutely not! But I gained a lot just by simply focusing on what really matters.

Risk Takers Get Places

TRUTH IS...
THIS IS ONLY for those who aren't afraid to believe that the power is within you!

You can take 1 million classes go to a thousand seminars and read hundreds of how to books but at the end of the day you still need the power within you to believe that you could do exactly what those other successful entrepreneurs did to get to where they are!

My story is so different from your typical success story because I simply learned 90% of what I know just by giving things a try.

TRY THIS: Build your brand around you and not others! Successful stories allow you to brand your empire, your story, so be as authentic as possible!

What I learned is, the realer you are the more people connect with you! The more people that connect with you the more that will start trusting you – and whatever it is that you represent they will support!

Because your relationship with your consumers are that powerful! Anything that your name is on they are going to follow which not only makes you successful financially but you mean something to others that will carry a lot value in your life and career.

TRUTH IS...
I am everything under the sun but who I really am! And it's okay because I get it now. So I just brush it all off and continue to work hard! Your focus should only be on being a better you for you and not what others have said or think about you.

Remember: What others feel, talk, or think about you has absolutely nothing to do with you! That's none of your business. Your business is to grow your business.

TRUTH IS…
Just because you may feel like you are better don't mean go be snobby towards them! You never know who you might save just by being nice, how good you make them feel!

    For the record they have benefits; a study paycheck, and could work their way up to the top just to name a couple! It's never where you work but how hard you work to reach goals!

TRUTH IS...
IF YOU'RE NOT SLEEPY
Get up clean the house
Fold clothes
Read a book
Write down more plans
CREATE OR
Add something to your vision board
Talk with God

Always Go That Extra Mile

TRUTH IS...
It doesn't matter if you are working for yourself or someone else! Going that extra mile matters. just doing what you are required to do on a job will leave you stuck in that position a little while longer than going that extra mile! Just doing what you are paid to do won't cut it! Being successful takes a lot of effort. In order to prepare yourself for your own business, you need to respect the business you are at. Having that "so what this isn't my shit" OR "long as I do what I'm paid to do" will never cut it.

In order to build respectful business relationships, relationships you will need to grow your business, you will need to go that extra mile.

Your Brand

TRUTH IS...
Your brand should tell a story.

You being the story teller.

Support comes from people who feel they know you. You and your brand has to be relatable, liked, and understood.

This would separate you from the rest. This would make your brand standout. Your brand should never have a limit on what it should be!

Anything you put your brand name on, you should be able to sell. Customers want to feel like they are a part of something great. Your brand is a movement. What does it represent. What type of people does your brand attract?

Your logo, down to the colors you choose, for your brand matters!

Move In Silence

TRUTH IS...

SOMETIMES WE GET so excited about our ideas, and all the success we know that's about to come with it! We start to share.

Next thing you know everything starts to go wrong! You feel so much pressure because you have already shared and now you feel obligated to continue. That turns into stress because now you're worrying about what others are going to think! Don't speak so soon! Grind now and explain later.

> *The truth is, women can do anything they want.*
> *There is absolutely no limit on what we can achieve,*
> *and I hope that every young woman*
> *approaches life that way. We can become even more successful*
> *if we support each other, empower each other, and mentor the*
> *next generation so they can stand on our shoulders."*
>
> -MICHELLE OBAMA

Work Ethic

TRUTH IS...
START RISING AND grinding in the morning like you're about get put out of your home.

There's something about struggling as a child that changes you. As I talk to God I always ask, "why me". Not as it relates to anything bad that happened, but for all the awesome things He's allowed me to see, do, and experience. I was a woman-child. I understood things way earlier than I should have been able to even process. When I see people struggling and seriously ok with "barely making it" I can only shake my head and then I raise it and say "but God".

The way my brain works I can't imagine doing the same thing and expecting a different result. But I have personally watched hundreds of individuals do it and it happens at every level – from extreme poverty to upper middle class. The actions are the same in terms of what lead people to these situations, but the results are different only based on support and access.

We were poor so, I knew nobody was going to save me from anything. Therefore, I worked and knew I had to work harder if I wanted anything. So, if you are reading this book and you are half-a$$ doing any and everything. I suggest you make this your last day operating that way. This book is for those that dream and do. I don't want anybody getting my little nuggets and wasting them on a hope and a prayer. Prayer changes things, but it won't change a thing if you're still out here cuttin' up.

So, the wrap up here is this:

Energy is everything. It's time for some of you to change your circle and go after what it is you truly desire for your life.

Class

TRUTH IS...
Class is an aura of confidence that is being sure without being cocky. Class has nothing to do with money. Class never runs scared. It is self-discipline and self-knowledge. It's the SWAG that comes with having proved you can meet life.

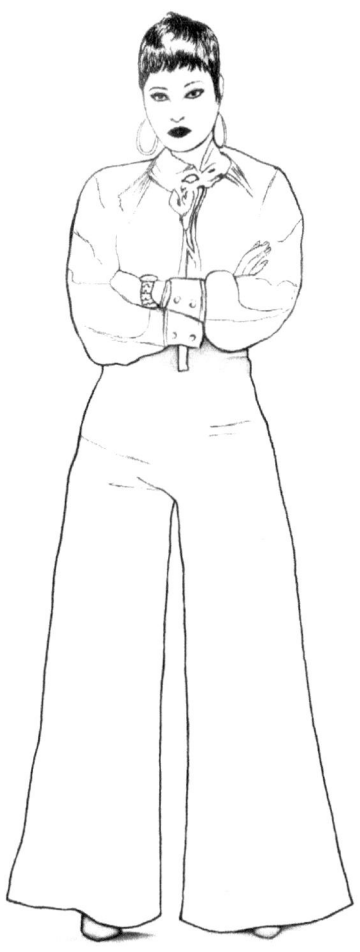

Reap And Sow

TRUTH IS…
THERE IS A reaping season & a sowing season. If you don't want your enemy's harvest don't sow the same seeds they sowed.

There are some people whose destiny is tied to yours & they're counting on you. So you can no longer afford to take or carry baggage, hurt, disappointment, distractions, people who look like sheep but underneath are wolves, or anything of the sort anymore. It's game time.

Practice is over. The devil is always going to fight us. That's what he does. But Do you care? No? Ok, then. Just do this.

Prayer

God I don't always know your plan but I know it is perfect. In every test there is a testimony. I am peaceful on your word this morning, no weapon formed against me shall prosper and despite the negativity and judgment so many are quick to make I am thankful for a forgiving heart, a strong mind and your favor, mercy and grace. I am clear the trick of the enemy is nothing more than a distraction. The enemy/enemies have no power over me.

In Jesus name.
AMEN.

It's Okay To Drop People Off

TRUTH IS...
IF YOUR INNER circle sucks, eliminate the people who are bringing you down. If you can't eliminate them, you've got to accept what they can give you and let go of the rest. Having expectations and having them not be met is the quickest way to feel like a victim. Get your power back by realizing that it's nobody's job to support you or make you happy but yourself.

Evolution and growth are vital to your happiness and success. Never be afraid to change what doesn't feel good. You have the right to design your life to look exactly the way you want it to. There's nothing more fabulous than a woman reinvented.

TRUTH IS...
You don't just flip a switch one day and become happy. Happiness is a commitment, a challenge, and an inside job. Only YOU know exactly what it takes to feel good. Check in with yourself daily and ask yourself if you're truly happy. And if the answer is no, figure out what needs to change.

And then give yourself the gift of making it happen.

Millions Of Stars In The Sky

TRUTH IS…

I FIND IT fascinating that people often accuse others of thinking that they're better than everyone else when they're simply trying to better themselves.

If I had a dollar for every time someone called me "fancy", "bougie", or a "diva" in a patronizing way, well, I'd be much more of a fancy bougie diva than I am right now!

Never ever let anyone make you feel badly for striving to be your best self. If your personal evolution pisses someone else off, then it's a reflection of them. Never apologize for wanting to think better, act better, or be better. If the people around you can't understand and respect that, then it's time to surround yourself with better.

Reasons

TRUTH IS...

IT'S ALL FOR a reason and serves a purpose. In the midst of most of things that happen in your life you won't understand it. There will be things that happen and people that leave or betray you and you will not be able to wrap you head around what's happening.

I'll share this with you and I hope that some of you are in a space to receive this nugget.

Let it go!

And when I say let it go it's not meant to be cliché. I mean to truly allow the people and things that no longer serve you for the better to go away.

Don't chase things or individuals. The reason or the season for them to be in your life has passed. That doesn't mean you won't see them again, but realize there's some you won't and accept it for what it is and move forward.

When you keep moving, you make a decision to not live a life of "yesterday" and start to move towards your purpose and your passion; the world opens up to you in a different way. It's not that you won't miss people or situations, but your decision to want more for yourself and your mere existence is why you made the decision in that moment and why God allowed the decision to be made for you when you weren't quite ready to make it yourself.

The best lesson I've ever learned is that He'll never take anything from you that's for you!

Take The Shot

TRUTH IS ...
You just have to stay on the corner of Awesome and Bomb-diggity!

Nobody else is going to put you in a position to win, but you. If you don't think you're the absolute shit, then I can assure you that there's not many other people that will!

Putting yourself in a position to win doesn't make you arrogant or an opportunist. I'm a firm believer in, "you reap, what you sow." But, I'm also a firm believer in taking your shot every single time and not ever shortchanging yourself.

I'm all about us all winning and being successful. But, you will do the work and you must kill, if you plan on eating with me. The days are gone for riding another person's coattail. If you think you can do it better and deserve to make more money, then show me how gangsta you are and go out there and do it! You can't have it both ways.

The wrap up here is this: There's pecking orders in place for a reason. And if you want to be the Head (you know what) in charge then there's a cost for that spot and you got to earn and pay for it. 365 days a year. On that note I'm just going to finish plotting on how awesomesauce I plan on being because I didn't come this far to fail and neither did you.

"Next time you catch yourself speaking words that do not support your goals, simply silence yourself and remind yourself that life and death is in the power of the tongue.

You can either speak life into your goals and situation with a positive perspective, or you can speak death into them. Do not allow negative talk on your part, or others. Good or bad, you will have what you say. Your words are just that powerful"

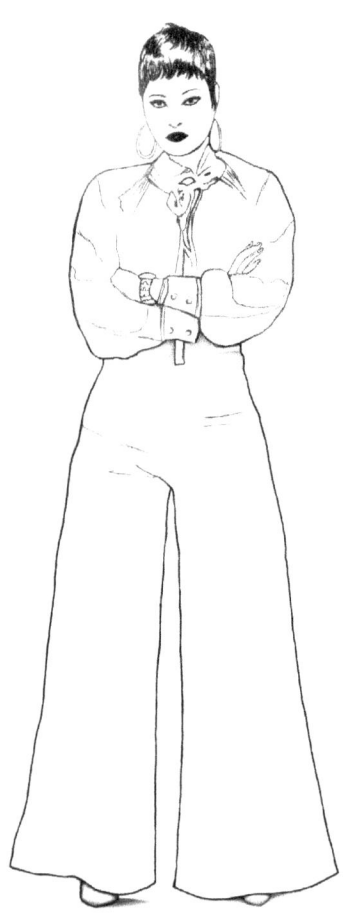

"Do not let your heart be troubled."

— John 14:1

TRUTH IS...
There's a reason, a season, and a purpose for it all. If we knew everything coming around the corner we'd never evolve into our best selves. That's sort of the price we pay to get to the next level.

The only reason I can share the things I do are because I've seen God's grace and favor more times in my life than one person deserves. No matter how awful or bad the situation seemed at the time. What He gave me in return was far better. Your flesh wants what it wants. But He will always give you what you need.

I've learned and grown much more through my failures and struggles than I ever had with any success. Every loss made me learn how to win! Abandonment and neglect gave me a heart and a spirit that became unbreakable. Depression made me understand what was important and taught me how to find happiness in the things that really matter.

So, the wrap up here is this: No matter how extra whack the situation may seem in this moment. Just know that we serve an in time God. What's waiting for you on the other side of your storm is a better life and a better you. But the only way over anything is to just go through it! Stay strong and find your center. Remember who you are and whose you are. Trust me on this one. He's got you.

TRUTH IS...
You thought Saturday's, rainy days, and sniffy sick days were days off? Oh sweet, sweet, love-bug, I'm going to need you to leave that old way of thinking back there with the wannabe bosses and pull yourself together, m'kay?!

I think I'm going to appoint myself as your virtual get-your-ass together fairy! I'll be that nagging voice that kind of rings in your ear when you know you need to be doing more, but you have more people around you than are being half-ass so when you think you're kind of killing it, but you're really not!

Truth IS

See, that's the trap! You haven't leveled up yet so, you can only see or even dream based on who and what you see the most.

Anything I've ever done was inspired by something else. I'm not artistic at all! I can't draw a straight line, but I'm creative in a different way. I know what I want, but more importantly, I execute my ideas! Knowing from whence I've come always offers me perspective. I know what it's like to have NOTHING! I know that when I had nothing at all I figured it out! So, if a 10-year old could figure it out, me and you can definitely get our shit together!

Life Is Short

TRUTH IS...

You know the saying, "life is too short", right? Well, it's not just a cliché, it's actually a fact. So many of us tend to forget how far we've come on the journey to finding our way that the busiest bee will appear out of nowhere and try to knock you off your A-game. It's easy to get sucked in and trust me, no matter how old you get, you still want to check people on site for even "trying you". You were simply minding your own business trying to actually accomplish what you set out to do, but nooooooo, they just must be busy!

Make Yourself Priority #1

TRUTH IS...

So, what I'll share with you is this! You can't do big shit! Go to great new heights! Expand your territory or grow your wealth getting caught up in things that don't really matter in the big scheme of things.

Feelings may get hurt from time to time, but as my therapist told me years and years ago, "they're just feelings"! Those three words changed my life. I learned to put them in their proper place and knew there was no way I could be the woman I was put here to be if I stayed in mine all the time. Life goes on and people tend not remember things in the way they actually happened.

I'm important to TONYA. She's my #1 priority! I'm going to make sure she's well taken care of before I try to take care of anybody or anything else. And what I've learned along the way is most people are out here doing the same so, once you know the rules of engagement you can govern yourself accordingly.

What you feed grows so, I'm just going full out and feeding greatness. Mediocrity and petty bullshit just can't reside in my brain space. Your mind is powerful. Use it wisely!

I'm rooting for you! Get your feelings in check because these feeling are going to keep you all broke. I'm on a paper chase so, I presently have zero time for that. I suggest you join me!

Don't Be A Doormat

TRUTH IS... FUCKKKKKKKKKKKKKKKKKKK!

Pardon my F-bomb but this is where you have to be in your mindset when you want to take yourself to another level! I can't tell you how many women I've coached over the last several years and all are successful in their own right, but for one reason or another they felt some form of guilt, uneasiness or whatever about putting their foot down and being clear with others about fees or boundaries or something!

You can't be a boss and a gentle delicate flower at the same time. You can't be around here trying to make friends with everyone that you want to do business with. So you're afraid to be clear about what it is you want and what you charge. If the relationship isn't mutually beneficial be very clear that you will have to have conversations up front. There's no room for a bunch of back and forth or gray areas.

As a woman in business you're going to have to be what some would consider a bitch sometimes. Just so we're clear, you're not being a bitch at all. They're just not accustomed to a woman asking for exactly what they want and getting it without a bunch of haggling!

So, the wrap up here is this... You have to be ok with others not being ok with your decisions. As long as you know that you're making decisions that are best for the way you need to do business and you've spelled everything out! That's it! I'm not in the convincing business. I hold not hostages and I release people to their destiny and know that whatever is for me is mine so, I stopped running after people for a dollar decades ago! Try it! You can thank me later! Maybe this was inspired by the Women's Equality Day that I failed to post about a couple of days ago!

Women having rights means nothing if we don't do anything with them.

Choices

TRUTH IS...

THE INSOMNIA SOME nights are too real but are totally self-inflected When the alarm sounds at 6:45am I have nobody to blame, but TONYA. I played myself. Life is about choices and this particular day I chose an afternoon nap and I knew it would come back to haunt me, but I made my bed!

The same goes for the tough hard choices and the huge decisions you'll face as you take yourself to another level. Sometimes you won't have a sounding board. There will be moments when nobody wants to hear your next new great idea. You have to learn that as an entrepreneur you'll have to go it alone! Get comfortable with being uncomfortable. It's not easy, but it's necessary to build your mental muscle.

Unconditional Love

TRUTH IS...

September is always an extra shitty month for me or at least it used to be! I have a made up mind this year that I will not be in a low grade depression missing my favorite person that has ever walked this earth. I really thought about it and it was an a-ha moment! My granny never had one day to mourn or cry or be sad about anything.

Most people thought she was mean because she had resting face on lock, but to me she was a total mush. I could do no wrong. I'm so glad she saw fit to take care of me, but I'm even more grateful that she loved me.

The kind of love she gave me was unconditional and life changing altering. Motherless daughters have a hard way in life and I know my life could have been totally different. But, my grandmother was not having a minute of that foolishness! For every mistake she made with my mom she did right by me. She never said I love you. I never heard those words in my house my entire life. But I totally felt loved and that's truly all that matters. It's because of her that words mean nothing to me.

Don't tell me you love me, but treat me like a stranger. Don't tell me you'll do anything and don't because I ask nothing of anybody. I was taught to depend on myself. But if you say it you better mean it! Because I know that people make time and money for anything they want in life so, if you want to have me in yours you better be ready to back up any and everything you say. I hate that character trait and it's because I saw her accept so little when she deserved the world.

Game Time

Truth IS

Truth is…

GET IN THE game and off the sidelines or get the hell out of my way. It's your decision! Nobody is forcing you to greatness no more than they are in your way to succeed or fail.

But what I need for some of you to realize is that this is not a game. This is real life tried and true. There isn't a whole lot new going on. The rules have been the same since the beginning. Eat what you kill! Keep playing if you want to!

Truth Hurts, Truth Heals

TRUTH IS...

I'M JUST HERE to give you a not so gentle nudge that quietly whispers in your ear, "get your ass in gear"! Think of me as your fairy sweet Auntie that really wants the best for you, but is about over you with all your excuses.

Cost is not always about money, but it is always about time, patience and determination. Those costs aren't tangible, but must be used often and regularly when trying to achieve anything.

You wonder why some people make it in one industry and some don't. You wonder why some people are still in the same situation they were after the market crashed almost eight years ago. Because they don't understand that there's a certain cost that must be paid to be the boss – and the rent is due daily.

Resting on what you did yesterday, last month or even last year aren't apart of the game plan when you have new money and new relationships. Old money, they can take a few more hits when things come crashing down. They have deeper relationships and more people to advise them on how to handle tough markets and adjust accordingly.

They have advisors! You don't! So get yourself together and make your own way. When you figure it out, build a network of people and get around others that don't only want to flash and talk about money, but those that want to figure out how we can make more money.

There's a price to pay when you level up. Do you negotiate? Absolutely! But to think that any and all knowledge will be free is doing yourself a great disservice and wasting a bunch of your time. Pay for what you want so you can get what you want.

If you have a service, you better charge for it as well! Talking to people that aren't going to execute 85% of the time, for free, is a waste of your time. At least if you were paid for your intellectual property you wouldn't feel bad!

There's more than one way to skin a cat! It's called multiple streams of income!

It's Saturday Though, So What?

Truth IS

TRUTH IS...

It's SATURDAY AND that means absolutely nothing to an entrepreneur except "let's get this money!" I challenge you to do better. I challenge you to push yourself. If your phones aren't ringing and customers aren't filing through the doors and you aren't spending a dime on advertising to get them there then I suggest you stay off social media and get online to take a few extra classes and learn a few tricks.

Beat the pavement if you must! It's your business. If you want people to know about it, you need to work more days than Monday - Friday to get the job done. Networking is more than going to events it's letting every person you come in contact with know that you have a business and you'd love for them to come by and visit your location and refer a friend as well. Having a business is a lifestyle, it's not a job. It takes focus and sacrifice to make it work. You get what you give and if you think you're the only person out here that's working and executing I assure you, you're sadly mistaken. You doing what has to be done to keep your doors open is expected. Having a sign, a space and some business cards doesn't make you a boss.

Social media is a great platform if used properly, but if you think it's a reflection of a person's entire life and how they live I think you need to take a hiatus. Stop being an internet troll and start using the information at your fingertips as fuel to set a fire under your own ass. It's timeout for games and coulda, woulda, shoulda's. Stop clogging your brain space with negativity and things and matters that add zero value. When you start really crushing it, I'll be the first one to clap and give you a high-five. But if you just want to keep talking and you can't pull the trigger on one idea and execute.... I'm not your girl and I'm not here for that!

Nobody Cares

TRUTH IS...

LET ME SHARE with you the best kept nugget in the entire world! And I'm going to need you to listen to me with your good ear. Ready?

Let me be very, very, clear... NOBODY CARES!

Your mess can be your message and your pain will have a purpose only if you make a decision to allow yourself to use it before it uses you! The last several weeks have allowed me to have coaching calls and one-on one sessions that made me see things in a different way.

When you're in the frame the picture is irrelevant. When you're in the forest the trees are merely a part of the backdrop.

So, what I'll share with you is this, It's you against you! Not the outside noise. Not the people that you thought loved you, but betrayed you! It's just YOU!

Mother's leave their children. Your blood relatives will turn on you like a stranger. But, at the end of the day it's YOU and how you respond that will dictate the way your story unfolds. It's YOU and the desires of your heart that will quit telling yourself that you're not worthy of anything less than the best! It's YOU that won't allow somebody else's floor to be your ceiling!

So, the wrap up here is this: Put yourself in a position to win and make no apologies for it. If others don't see how awesome-sauce you are... fuck 'em! Sorry, for the F-bomb, but not really! Seriously, F--k'em! You have to fight for the best life you think you deserve and at the end of the day...It's YOU against YOU! Make sure you WIN!

Birds Of A Feather Flock Together

TRUTH IS...

> "Birds of a feather flock together. If you run around with losers you will end up a loser, unconsciously. You will pick up their ways, pick up their habits, and most important will pick up their attitude about life. If you are around cynical and negative people all the time, you will become cynical and negative. So you have to watch yourself. allow yourself with powerful people who can encourage you, who can lift you up. People who are doing what you want to do. People who want more in life and seeking higher ground in life."
>
> – LES BROWN

TRUTH IS ...

WHAT'S SO CUTE about a group of toxic chicks Drinking, smoking, Instagramming, lurking, and gossiping? Be a little more mindful of the company you keep, negative toxic people can get in your way of becoming great! Spirits and energy do rub off! Once you remove these kind of people out your life watch how the creator instantly start pouring blessings upon you!

Elevation

TRUTH IS...

I was a hot mess thinking I was all that! I didn't have shit together but the slay I was wearing in my head! You will be surprised how many women could relate to your bullshit! But until they become truthful with themselves they will forever be stuck in that shell. Once you accept your shit you will start cleaning it up! Don't be ashamed your story could help someone out!

Listen, for a very long time I was the underdog! I was you. That person who struggled through everything! School, Business, Self-worth, you name it! For a very long time I didn't think I was worthy of anything! I was attacked, judged, talked about, etc. I was quiet for a very long time!

Anywhere I went I wouldn't talk. I was so insecure with who I was I thought the world could see that, everything I ever gained someone downplayed it or tried to get it taken away from me! The things I lost were broadcasted. I was so broken!

LET ME TELL YALL SOMETHING!

Anything I write about is to motivate you all. I know what failure, discouragement, and insecurity feels like. Take me for an example that God has the last say so! No matter what a person wishes upon you, no one is as powerful as God! don't let anyone tell you differently about me or yourself! I represent y'all! So I try to do it well. Nothing I have define who I am, my character does.

Power In The Tongue

TRUTH IS...
CHANGE YOUR SURROUNDINGS! Letting people speak negativity into your spirit is not a good thing. And you wonder why things aren't working out. (It's always something) isn't it! the first thing you say when things don't go your way whole time it's so much mess around you there's no room for growth.

Build Meaningful Relationships

TRUTH IS...
A SMART PERSON knows better!

Building relationships with other important, smart, known people is way better than trying to be better than them join them so you all will be great together. Market yourself right because you can be easily seen as negative and that will never be good for your business your brand!

It's better to love than hate. Hate could put a chokehold on your life and place your mind in a dark place

My flaw is trusting. What's yours?

_____
_____
_____
_____
_____

TRUTH IS...
Get up and take care your business even if it's just cleaning up or sorting out papers & bills. GET UP. Don't let the devil get all up in your ear. Fight it off.

I know things could be so stressful and overwhelming at times but the great part is this as soon as you're ready to change your situation you can! By simply getting up and getting started.

Nobody has ever told me what I'm telling you all. I can't imagine what some of you are going through without support and inspiration.

So here it is,

Get up and get your shit in order. You can do it! I know you can because I did!

Truth

DON'T YOU KNOW some people that are following you or stalking your page on social media actually HATE YOUR ASS. No matter how nice and positive you are some people will never ever like you and damn sure don't wish you well.

Do you know some people have mastered the art of trying to fuck up a person's life? I know sometimes you want to stunt as soon as you hear good news but just wait until you know for sure that it's a go! Some people are praying on your downfall and some of them creepy MFer's are going to go buy candles and incense and shit. Tell God if you want to tell somebody!

Get You A Mentor

TUTH IS...
MENTOR - AN EXPERIENCED and trusted advisor.

The reason I call myself experienced is because I teach people to not make the same mistakes I did. I learned so much from my mistakes. Everything I failed at, everything that has ever happened to me I learned from. You can never get advice from a person who never went through or experienced the things you have.

It blows people minds when I tell them I have no manager or no marketing team.

I learned everything through the streets instead I added a twist a LEGAL twist to it! And now I'm making over 6 figures.

I've learned so much about the business and found a new love in helping others. Watching someone else grow as a person and in business.

Small Steps Are Still Progress

TRUTH IS...
Ever looked on someone else and feel like your life suck?

WELL STOP THAT SHIT!
If you know that every day you give what it takes to move forward in whatever dreams or goals you have for yourself and are working hard to achieve them, then that's all that matters.

Look at the small steps you're making to be just as dope, just as fit, just as fly, just as positive, just as successful, and say to yourself,

"EVEN ON MY WORST DAY IM STILL KILLING IT"

Because guess what? That one small step you called the worst day ever, matters! No matter what the chick or dude over there doing! Don't worry about them! Cause guess what? They might be watching you and feeling the same way.

A positive and confidence mind attracts opportunities. Pat yourself on the back no matter how small your day was. Every day counts!

TRUTH IS...
I'm a believer in energy, energy travels! You attract what you are! I'm afraid of people, I'm afraid of their intentions! I also don't believe everyone deserves my friendship or my presence! Once I see your circle is NOT progressive I remain distant! But I will still love you! I overly value myself therefore I don't allow too many different spirits around me! People who give away their friendship so freely don't value it! Friendships should be earned, you can't pick friends because they got a cute face and some followers it's deeper than that.

TRUTH IS...
When people from the past try to get back in your life, but you're no longer on those old thought patterns, you're no longer wasting your time and energy on meaningless activities with them. You're no longer trying to get approval from

them, because you approve yourself. You're no longer trying to fit in, because you realized your self-worth. You're no longer interested in their negativity, because you know that time is precious and you want to focus on being the best that you can be. So you hit them with that "new mindset, who dis" reply, because you're no longer who you use to be. "Allow me to reintroduce myself" is your new mentality, because your growth game is strong. You just know, that you know, because you ain't looking back.

TRUTH IS…
Focus on that one small step you can take first. There's always time to make a change and strive for more. You can't choose what life throws at you, but you can choose how you respond to it. Start somewhere, Start NOW! It doesn't really matter what other people think you should be doing with your life. All that matters is that YOU know what you're doing with your life.

> *I know where I'm going and I know the truth, and I don't have to be what you want me to be. I'm free to be what I want.*
>
> — MUHAMMAD ALI

I CAN. YOU CAN. WE CAN!
Focus on you.

Seeds Planted

Tonya R

TRUTH IS...

NOT TOO LONG ago I planted squash in my back yard. Spring came, summer came, fall came and winter came. It never blossomed. This year I started my garden in my back yard again and I decided not to plant any squash. As March and April approached I noticed that there was squash growing in the front of my house. How was that? Well birds had picked my seeds up from last year and dropped them in my front yard. They are growing like crazy now. The moral of the story is this! Keep planting seeds (exposing your business and your brand to more and more people) it may not blossom right then and there when you expect it to but the seeds will spread, the word will get around and your harvest will grow! No one can stop that.

Ego, The Loud Killer

TRUTH IS…

AFTER YOU SACRIFICE your ego you will begin to spiritually evolve in ways you never imagined. You will begin to shed bad energies and the people who carry bad energy. Your higher self will only attract the people that have the energy you need and crave to elevate you to your highest self. You will walk away from all the people who has been stealing your energy for years with no apologies! During this process you might feel lonely but you're never alone. Your guides, Angels and Ancestors will be will you leading you to your true self! Trust the process of knowing Thy Self.

Popular Or Wealthy

TRUTH IS…
Boss 101

As a Boss, a CEO, and an Entrepreneur it is your duty every day to wake up and say to yourself "I'm going to make more money than I spend today" And stick to it!

I don't care if you are just starting a business or had your business for years. This is mistake I see happen pretty often. In order to be successful you cannot hustle backwards! If you have money to blow than cool but if you're on a mission to become extremely successful then you must have this mindset. For example, I know how hard it is to have millions of people doing what you're doing not because they have a love for it but simply because they feel there is money in it. They may feel they could be on the level that you are on. So some of us go spend tons of money to stay on top!

But if you're smart you could do so many things without having to spend all your money doing so. And still be on top!

Everything you do should have a budget and everything you do could also be negotiated!

I don't go home unless I make money and everything I do in business has to:

1. Make me money
2. Make sense

Simple enough?

If someone is inviting you to do something with them and they are getting paid for it then you should be getting paid as well!! It's cool to be famous and popular but also got to get paid!

TRUTH IS ...
Never downplay what you worked hard for just to please people who never going to like or support you anyway!

It's not you, your success, or what you post about every day they hate! It's the fact that you are doing what they wish for!

But the volume of hate they have for you is so damn loud they can't hear what God is trying to tell them about themselves!

Maybe if they turn it down just a little they can hear him speak! God is trying to tell you something! He is spitting game to you! Showing you which way to go! You keep missing it!

TRUTH IS...
It is much easier to visualize your accomplishments by writing them down. I don't care how small they are. This would allow you to start appreciating yourself more instead of looking at someone else life and felling like you are not doing enough If you got up today and started on something that's a step.

Let's be honest

Truth is...

WOMEN LIE ABOUT allot of things. We lie about our age, size, weight, and number of sexual partners. We often pretend that we are fulfilled sexually when we are not. We avoid telling our girlfriends the truth about their appearance...that they need to update their hairstyle, makeup and overall look. We seldom make the time to tell the people we love that they have wronged us, disappointed us or hurt us, yet we feel justified in carrying a grudge against them for years. The truth is that women in general have a difficult time understanding and communicating our truth for fear of hurting the people we love.

Here are a few facts that I've learned about truth:

1. The truth is good enough.
2. The truth will set you free.
3. The truth holds you (and others) accountable.

Learning to embrace my truth has been a long, difficult journey. But I can honestly say that once I made peace with the fact that my relationships DESERVED my truth, my life changed. Because prior to my revelation, I always held back because I didn't feel my relationships could survive the truth and I didn't want to hurt the people I loved. But then an angel said to me that truth doesn't destroy relationships, the lack of truth does. And any relationship that couldn't survive my truth wasn't worth saving.

You will always have surface, meaningless relationships if you don't commit to being honest with those who are close to you. Please don't misunderstand my point, there is something to be said for delivery and timing, but when you love someone (and when they love you) you owe them the opportunity to know your truth. Let's set a new standard in our relationships that includes being wholly honest with others and ourselves! I promise you that your life will change for the better when you grant yourself permission to share your truth, good, bad or indifferent!

Let's continue to be honest...

TRUTH: The pill that everyone wants to prescribe for others, but are seldom willing to swallow themselves. Women love to shed light on the lies men tell but the truth is that we tell lies too! The business of truth works both ways we have to be just as willing to "hear" the truth of others, as we are to "speak" our truth to others. I can own up to the fact that I didn't always receive truth from my loved ones in the past because I made it very difficult for them to be honest with me. Experience has taught me that I do not have editorial control over truth; I cannot change it at will because I don't agree with or like what is spoken. We have to be careful of what we ask for at times because we only "think" we want truth when in fact, some truths are better left unknown. Some of us convince ourselves that we desire truth when we are not ready or prepared for the responsibilities that accompany knowledge and awareness. I was no exception to the rule.

Honestly speaking, there are certain realities that I wish I could unknown. This is the obvious risk associated with demanding truth. But I have no regrets because the hard truths in my life is what brought about change. My growth point here was learning to share truth with respect and consideration and receive truth with acceptance and love regardless of the circumstances.

So my advise to anyone who has a difficult time with the business of truth is simple:

The next time you decide to call any man, woman or child on the carpet for lying, make certain that you hold yourself to the very same standard of truth! Always remember...being willing to speak the truth is only one part of the equation. We must also be willing (and prepared) to hear the truth without judgment, blame or defense.

I understand the fact that you can't make a difference telling people only what they want to hear. Sometimes we have to make room for TRUTH!

Be An Example

TRUTH IS...

When you lead it's important you lead by example! This is for all my website small business owners. If you have a website, you know what a dashboard is. People call me "erky" because I post all day every day. Long posts, short posts, just POST, POST, POST! If you don't, how will the world know you? How will your new followers know what you do? Are you going to leave it up to them to figure it out? Not everyone scrolls down your page! So you must advertise your business! Make sure your site is up and running and the link is on every network you have! Be smart! If you're going to use social media get paid for it! But don't let this fool you I am broke, all of my money goes back into my businesses I don't use my money to stunt I want to help everyone reach success even my haters!

Focus

TRUTH IS…
See how far you can go! Fuck what the person next to you, behind you, or even in front of you is doing! Create a path for yourself! Stay there and do some remarkable shit! Surprise yourself see how far you can go.

Then KEEP GOING! See, y'all have to get crazy with this business shit. Y'all have to start going dumb hard. In a positive way, nothing cutthroat or shady.

Just start believing you can do it all and then actually do it! Be so Tasmanian people get out your way when they see you! Cause they key to your own success is not looking at anybody, just focusing on what it is you're doing.

I don't watch anybody else and I don't hear shit! Stay in tune with what you are doing! Find your rhythm and rock to your own beat! And when you come to watch how much progress you see in yourself! And nobody will have to tell you! You will see it.

TRUTH IS…
You know the saying "what you hang around is what you become"? Stop being jealous, envious, and intimidated by the people who are ahead of you. Appreciate the fact you are around someone who can teach you how to become a better you!

These type of people are motivators and blessings! Think a little deeper then jealousy & envy but sit back ask for tips and take notes! Stop being fearful of someone being better then you that turns into so much that distract you from being who God really created you to be!

Sit your pride to the side, get that shade out your heart, and start winning! Winners don't have pride! We are very fearful people.

TRUTH IS...

I don't care how good your product is! If a person is not getting respect and appreciation from your business they will take their money elsewhere! Apologizing to a customer is highly appreciated, if something in your business didn't go as planned! People are understanding to situations if you communicate with them!

You and your team has to be on the same page if the level is off by an inch someone has to go!

One wrong move and it could all go downhill! Be cautious of the decisions you make in your business.

TRUTH IS…
It is much easier to be nice to others than treating people like you are better than them. This makes people like you which now turn them into supporters. Now you have your supporters attention it is your duty to show them how to be successful like you. Come up with something others can also make money from. Remember, it's not all about you. Them same people are going to spread the word about you which brings you more strangers that turn into friends then customers now you have NEW ambassadors who will eventually bring you more strangers

TRUTH IS…
Sometimes you have to be quiet and just listen.

Being a boss or a leader doesn't always means taking the lead controlling every situation. Sometimes you have to fallback and allow others to get their shine on!

One person doesn't know everything that's why teams are often times stronger than one

Nothing Grows In Your Comfort Zone

TRUTH IS…

YOU HAVE TO become comfortable with being uncomfortable. Having set hours and a day that's planned with no disruptions will not be the life you want to lead if you actually want to accomplish anything significant.

As a child, I had to be ok with being teased about the way I talked, the way I walked, and even why I was always doing "too much"! I wanted to do the things that I liked and that was cheering and being involved. That made a lot of people very uncomfortable.

"Who does she think she is"…those six words will make or break a young person.

I thank God for His grace. I thank my Uncle for helping me drown out the noise. I thank my younger self for realizing early on that my situation was temporary if I made it so.

That was years ago but those same things motivate me today. When I see people tear each other down because they're not brave enough to go after whatever it is they say they want today I want to slap them with a wet open hand! Grow up! They are adults, but they act just like children from deplorable environments that don't know any better. But they're no longer children and the only person they should be mad at is themselves. But no, they choose to rain on your parade and tell everybody else what they can or can't do!

Cut those people off and move forward to your best self. Slackers and losers only project their insecurities and shortcomings on you because they need a squad to make them feel like they've actually done something with their life. That's not your job and that's not the group you want to join so skedaddle!

You've entered a new phase of your life and it's the kind of the lightbulb moment for you so, just be prepared to walk some miles of this journey alone.

Truth IS

Initially you'll miss the dumb ass conversations you used to have with them, but you're about to be so busy kicking total ass in these streets you'll learn being #1 requires extra determination, sacrifice and distance. Most people don't have that in them so, it's best you limit your time with them anyway if you actually want to do what you came here to do!

Trust The Process

TRUTH IS...
IN ORDER TO become who God created you to be, you must endure the process!

I couldn't go around my process; I had to go through it!

TRUTH IS...
My faith is what keeps me going even when I feel too tired to keep moving. Even when I want to succumb to the pressure, I keep in mind that I was made for this. I was built to last. I was created to change the lives of many. It gets hard, and often times I don't know what to do, but I keep going. That's the key. Always keep going. Always keep pressing. Always keep dreaming. One day you're going to wake up on the other side of the dream and you'll be living it

TRUTH IS...
You can make a lot of money but the wrong mindset will keep you broke. You can get a lot of opportunities but the wrong mindset will keep you from getting the right opportunities. Some of you aren't where you could be because your mind simply ain't right. Get your mind where it needs to be and watch how things start lining up. Here's a sobering thought for you:

> *Your life looks exactly how you thought it would look. Change your mind and it'll change your life.*

TRUTH IS

I'm just trying to put people in a position to elevate their lives through my tests that turned into learning testimonies. I've elevated my life completely and my tax bracket and Thanks to God I am willing to keep going!! I support who support me. No hype. One of the many lessons I've learned is LIFE goes on with or without YOU! All things aren't what they seem. I'm forever a student of life!

Fixed Identity

TRUTH IS...

WE ALL HAVE to work on starving the ego. Sometimes we become SO attached to ideas that they literally start to define who we are. This is called our FIXED IDENTITY. We are so attached to this identity that we refuse to consider anything that doesn't reaffirm those ideas we have about ourselves and how things "should be." This includes religion, cultural norms, the food we eat, etc.

That is called ego clinging. We cling in an attempt to feel good about who we are. The funny part about this is we start to see others who correct us, debate us or ruffle our feathers as people we dislike. Why? Because they are forcing us to reexamine our beliefs. They make us feel uncomfortable. Don't be so attached to an idea that it upsets you when someone else has another idea. We ALL have to work on this.

Thoughts Become Things

TRUTH IS...

IF YOU WANT to prosper, you must use prosperity thinking. To help you do this, here are some prosperous affirmations to practice:

> My income is constantly increasing.
>
> I prosper wherever I turn.
>
> Today is a delightful day. Money comes to me in expected and unexpected ways.
>
> I give myself the green light to go ahead, and to joyously embrace the new.
>
> Green means "go," and I choose to go for all the good life has in store for me.
>
> I love dress-up holidays. I can be anyone I choose today.
>
> I support others in becoming prosperous, and in turn, Life supports me in wondrous ways.
>
> I am now willing to be open to the unlimited prosperity that exists everywhere.
>
> I live in a loving, abundant, harmonious universe, and I am grateful.
>
> I deserve the best, and I accept the best now.
>
> All is well and I am safe.

Half Love

Truth IS

"Half lovin just hurts."

– Will Smith

When we say we love someone we should give all we've got, even if that means overcoming the parts of ourselves that keep us from the best parts of ourselves that deliver the promise of ecstatic love. Not only do we deserve to experience the best of who we are, but also the people who we say we love deserve to experience the best of WHAT we are.

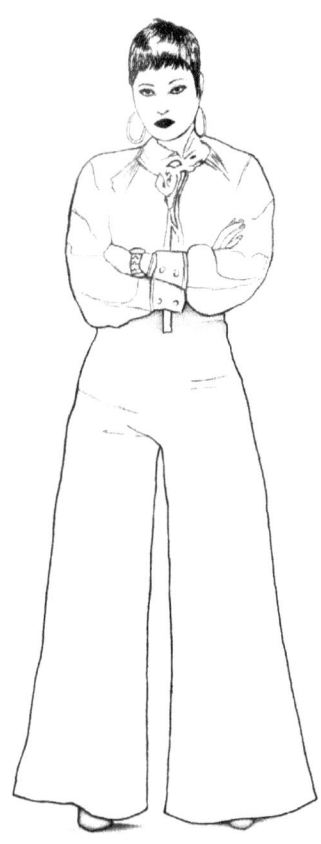

Straight Up, No Chasing

TRUTH IS...

DON'T EVEN RUN the risk of falling for the wrong person. How about not even giving them 1 minute of your time. I've never known anyone to pick the wrong person and not see the signs beforehand! You are way too special to waste your precious time. Also, you could be spending time with the wrong person when the right one comes along! It would be a shame for you to miss it due to straight foolishness!

All things work together for the good of those that love The Lord!

God will use the good, bad, and the ugly to get you there! Trust Him & ENDURE!

Some people will never be to you what you are to them! Changing your expectations will reduce your disappointment!

God has to remove the wrong people so that He can make room for the right people. Don't ever chase anybody down to be a part of your world. If they don't know, let those jokers go! You are too fabulous to beg.

TRUTH IS...
Parents, tell your children how wonderful, smart, beautiful & awesome they are - if you don't tell them they'll never believe it!

TRUTH IS...
Live with no regrets! If you change one thing, then everything changes. Know that you are exactly where you're supposed to be!

TRUTH IS...
Men, stop telling us what you think we want to hear in order to get what you want, that's extortion!

    And ladies, use your heads not just your heart!

TRUTH IS...
Know that whatever you do to get him, that is what you will have to do to keep him! Don't put your best foot forward to the degree that you can't back it up and sustain it.

If you cooked every night to get him then guess what? You'll be cooking all week!

BE WISE ladies! Maybe cook twice a week instead.

TRUTH IS...
A man will give you a clear view of your future with him and a commitment. Boys keep you guessing, waiting, wondering and are full of empty promises and games. You have to learn to separate the real from the BS.

My Life Choices

My life choices were slim:

- Choice #1: Go and get a 9-5 that would pay me $10/$16hr.

(Note: I quickly realized that I'd rather slit my wrist. The long way. So clearly, this idea was out).

- Choice #2: Marry a King Pin or Professional athlete.
    - Because I'm sort of from the hood and when I was young, that was my aspiration. The dope boys were our prince charming. And I wanted nothing more than to be a hustler's wife or basketball wife!

(Note: I am now painfully aware that a man is not a financial plan. So much for that bright idea!)

- Choice #3: Become an entrepreneur.
    - The thought of becoming an entrepreneur was my AHA! moment.

Entrepreneurship is what I was born for. But there were more obstacles. My skill sets were slim.

This is what I was good at:

Skill Set #1: The fight.
I spent my whole life fighting. Verbally, if you doubted me. And physically, if I felt like you wouldn't understand me any other way. But I always got my point across. One way. Or the other.

Skill Set #2: The Hustle.
I was raised by them. It's in my blood. This, I concluded, is what I was great at.

Skill Set #3: The writing.
I learned to master the art of writing in an awesome program called Anger Management in high school.

I knew how to fight for what I believed in. I was born to hustle. And my writing was pretty damn good. I had passion, drive, determination and all I needed were the customers to buy what I had to sell. And this is where the inspiration to write and self-published my first book, Grimey Enough, came from.

I had the burning desire to be an entrepreneur when everyone around me said that it wasn't possible. They said I didn't have what it took. And the odds? Well, they were stacked against me.

I saw my first five figure month that year. I was 24 years old and been living life on my own terms since. And finally knew what the ultimate revenge was….

It was called: <u>SUCCESS</u>.
So much for needing a degree. Hustle, I learned quickly, is the only skill you'll ever need!

Truth IS

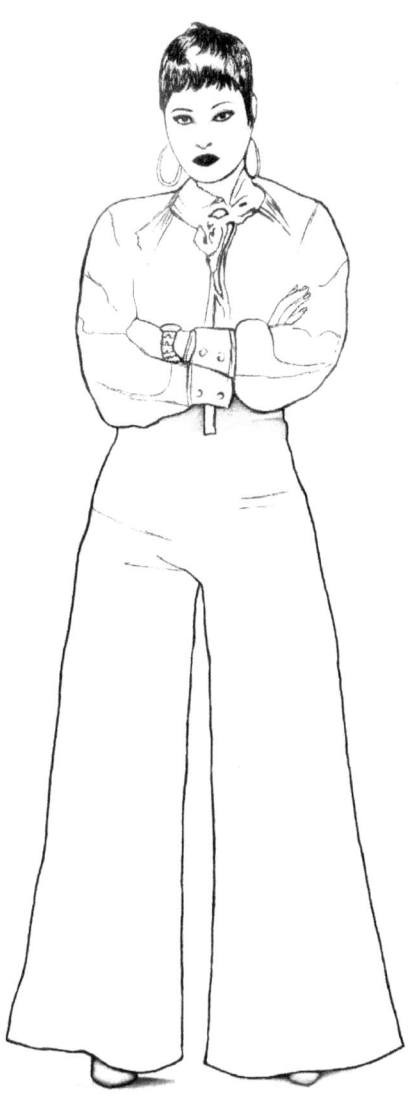

Think Big

TRUTH IS...

ONE MANTRA AND daily life practice I live by is THINK BIG! One of the biggest hang ups and stuck points of business owners is that they often think too small. What this does is hold you back from really taking the big leaps you need in order to get the big results.

Say the words "THING BIG" out loud.

Right now. Really, say it out loud and mean it!

Something happens when you do this in your body. When you are thinking BIG, your roadblocks begin to fall away in your mind and you make room for all of the big ideas to seep into world.

What's your mantra (s)?
_____
_____
_____
_____
_____
_____
_____
_____
_____
_____
_____
_____
_____
_____
_____
_____!
_____

I Wanna Start A Business, But Im Broke

TRUTH IS...
I HAD THAT same exact challenge. I didn't have enough money to even pay my own bills let alone start my own business. However, when I thought about it I realized that if I didn't have enough money to pay my bills now, how was I going to change it in the future?

I was tired of being behind, tired of scrambling, and I wanted more out of life so you know what I did? I found a way and I'm very grateful for my decision.

Let me ask you something, if you really felt this was the chance for you to get control of your financial future and have control over your life, do you think you could find a way to make it happen?

TRUTH IS...
Keep a journal. It not only helps you see what's working and what's not working, it's very therapeutic and it's one of the most valuable things you'll leave behind when you're gone.

Tonya R

The road to success is not straight. There is a curb called Failure, a loop called Confusion; speed bumps called Friends; red lights called Enemies; caution lights called Family. You will have flats called jobs. But, if you have a spare called Determination; an engine called Perseverance; insurance called Faith, and a driver called Jesus, You will make it to a place called SUCCESS!!!

—Unknown

Don't Do The Compete Thing

TRUTH IS…

Think about it ladies…when you are in competition with another woman you could only be trying to win something. Win what? A man? An award? A cookie? WHAT? Look at yourself as a prize then you will become that woman they are competing for. Keep in mind, a competitor can only win or lose, but the prize, "THE PRIZE", is what they are all competing for in the first damn place!

TRUTH IS…

Don't force things in life. If you keep pursuing something a relationship, a friendship, or the same business opportunity and you keep getting the same result, trust in God enough to know that it's not for you. God doesn't give us everything we ask for, for a reason. Maybe it's not the right time in our lives or maybe we wouldn't be able to handle it, who knows. Trust him anyway.

Closed Mouths Don't Get Fed

TRUTH IS…
EGO AND DOGGED pride can destroy you. Stop with the Lone Ranger syndrome! It's a myth! You don't ask for help because you're weak. You ask for help to remain strong. You cannot do it alone. And don't ever get your self-worth confused with your net-worth. Both are important, but one is useless without the other.

Always being offended is a sign of a lack of personal development…Being soft will leave you stuck just like fear will…Step up!

TRUTH IS…
Ladies need to stop living in fear! Being scared is why you stay in that no good relationship, dead end job, miserable situation! Put your fear to the side or stay stuck! There's power outside of your comfort zone!

Get Your Own

TRUTH IS…

LADIES, GONE ARE the days of men tricking because you're cute with a big butt. They want more. Substance, maturity, and independence are priceless assets! These dudes need your help more than ever because hustling isn't what it used to be.

Many graduates are out of work or underpaid and the ones who have child support issues need you to cosign on that car or apartment. You have more power than you give yourself credit for. It's an equal playing field so stop dreaming of meeting a man in the club who's going to give you the keys and security codes.

Shopping like the movie Pretty Woman, if you get lucky enough to even go shopping after meeting him the first night, will cost your soul. I'm willing to bet a stack that you sold your soul by sleeping him the first night you met him for that shopping trip.

These men are on to you acting independent but, truthfully, you have no money in your account. OH and gentleman, the ladies are on to your fronting asses too while you pop 4 bottles with 10 dudes and have no ladies in the section!

Being broke is a weakness and I want you all to be strong!

Guess What?

Tonya R

An 11-year-old black child has joined Mensa after scoring higher than Stephen Hawking, Bill Gates, and Albert Einstein on an IQ test. Ramarni Wilfred started showing signs of genius as a toddler, when his favorite book was an encyclopedia.

He could read and write by the time he started reception at school and last year, at the age of 10 and still in primary school, wrote a philosophy paper on fairness that earned him a 2:1 and a mock Oxford graduation. Prof. Hawking, Microsoft founder Gates and Einstein all have 160 IQs. Ramarni scored 162, putting him in the top 1% in the UK. Children hold the future. Like if you respect intelligence.

This really made me proud.

Cheating Is Hard Work

TRUTH IS...
Cheating is hard work.

Why? You have to keep deleting texts, keep locking your phone, keep deleting messages off of Facebook & Twitter. You find yourself spending way more money than you should trying to take care of two households, & Think of lies as to why you didn't come home.

That's too much for me! I'd rather be loyal! If you put such energy into that one person, finding ways to keep them happy, then life would be so much easier.

Gentlemen

TRUTH IS…
EVERY WOMAN WHO is nice to you does not want to sleep with you.

Every woman who reaches out to you, does not want to touch or be touched by you.

Lastly, every woman is not out to trap you, get you, or hurt you.

There are women who enjoy the company of a man, the intellectual conversation he may bring, the laughter two can share, and the honoring of two souls that happens with communication. Some of us enjoy the true beauty of a man's soul and can do so without complicating it, sexually.

Winners Never Quit, Quitters Never Win

TRUTH IS…
I have seen many people quit because things aren't as easy as they thought it would be and would downplay the lives of others who actually didn't.

People would come up with every story in the word of how another person got to where they are instead of admitting to the fact they were strong and bold enough to keep going no matter what the circumstances were.

People would actually try to come in your life at a time when God starts blessing you and think your blessings are supposed to roll right over to them without them going through or working hard like you did to get to where you are and would quit when they notice they "still have to work".

TRUTH IS…
WINNERS TAKE RISKS!
WINNERS SACRIFICE A LOT!
WINNERS HUSTLE WITH NO DAYS OFF!
WINNERS LOSE WITHOUT GIVING UP!
THEY JUST TRY AGAIN!

There's no easy way out! No matter where you are or where you're going you still have to work in order to become successful. I understand not everyone is supposed to be on top but the type to faith and belief I have in our Lord and Savior everyone sure as hell could be.

TRUTH IS…
You could be the total package!

Love yourself, believe in yourself, and trust God!

The feeling of being exactly what you post, living a life that's really yours, is one of the best feelings ever. It isn't all about money, clothes, and cars. But rather about faith, belief, & happiness.

Truth IS

Some people are successful but depressed and empty. Some people are broke and content with whom they are. But know God said you can be all things if you have faith and trust in him.

Tonya R

TRUTH IS…
You know that very moment when shit got real and things got tuff and you just couldn't take anymore so you said "F*** IT!" Not knowing that was your last test and your breakthrough was moments away!

So now you are at square one watching someone else do all the shit you know you could have done but you just couldn't take anymore.

There's something about a MONDAY. You are the least motivated on this day but understand you have people like myself who get it! We understand that faith has to be 24/7 so we're going to get it!

Please don't fold!Pressure and depression is a pain but I promise if you stay strong and stand firm you will be alright! I want to see you all win!

I am praying for everyone with a vision, everyone with a dream, and people who want more for themselves and their children. YES YOU CAN & YES YOU WILL! Just don't crack!

What Is A Shero To You?

A Shero is someone who makes a BIG impact on other people lives. She saves lives daily and does things selflessly. From a random hug, a simple smile, or a hello, she does many things to brighten up someone else's day. That is what makes her feel good inside.

A Shero takes nothing for granted! She truly knows her blessings came from God. She's a giver who gives without any doubt. Shero's don't look for anything in return. She fearlessly accepts every flaw, trial, and tribulation in her life. She uses her experiences to save others.

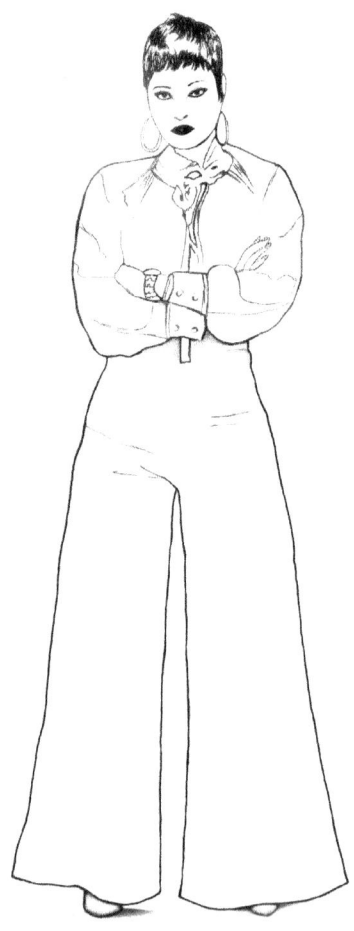

TRUTH IS...
I couldn't imagine taking what God has blessed me with and not sharing it with others! What I do for my community and the people who support me or call on me when needed isn't for show. I've been a giver all my life. It's just something that comes so naturally! To see our women support all these businesses and 80% of them businesses don't show the same love back makes me so sad. I was always told to take care the people who take care of you. Nothing I've done would be successful without you!

You have women out here that do and give so much. Just because they don't have a big following base on social media don't think they don't have money. People don't pay them homage which sucks because the same people you give your energy, your money, and pay homage to have never done what these women are out here doing!

Everything is about money and if that's what a Shero is to you then so be it. But that's not motivation to me.

A Shero to me is
_____
_____
_____
_____
_____
_____
_____
_____
_____
_____
_____
_____
_____!

They Said, "You Aint Gonna Make It"

TRUTH IS…
I CHOSE NOT to listen!

People were telling me " how are you going to keep up? All of those bills, all of that responsibility, how are you going to do it?"

People would say. "How are you going to make it work? I can't see it." So they wouldn't support it. Nobody really believed in me.

When things fell apart people were whispering, " I told you so!"

"What she gonna do now"

BUT I KEPT GOING!
Now everybody is asking me to put them on! Even if it's just for advice. I can't go a day without someone talking about me.

But they always follow behind with, "She's doing her thing though"

No matter how annoyed the haters and the doubters may make me feel for some odd reason the feeling always ends up feeling good at the end of my day. Because every night I find myself talking to God thanking him and everyday he reminds me how far I came.

The vision you have, that bubble in your stomach, the nervousness and fear you feel is God telling you that you're up next! So don't ignore it! I don't care who it is or who doesn't get it. It's not for them to understand!

I want to see you all WIN, even the ones that wish bad upon me!

Pick And Choose

TRUTH IS...
STOP PUTTING so much time and energy in the wrong things!

Some of you would much rather chase a man or woman around all day and all night and then when it's time to get up for work you get upset. That job is the one that's taking care you and your kids. You go to work with an attitude, you don't want to complete shit, or give it your all simply because you're upset.

Your job is your provider!

You have some business owners who won't take the time to invest into their business but would invest into a man or woman by buying shoes, bags, clothes or cars.

You would much rather take a gamble on a human then take a gamble on your business. That same business that's had been keeping you a float.

You have to love honor and protect the things that are taking care of you!

Give the most time to the things that are making sure you are straight.

I am married to my Business.

We have been taking care each other for so long! Now the world sees our growth.

When Friends Become Enemies

TRUTH IS...

UNDERSTAND WHEN A person is mad at you they will leave nothing out! But all those feelings have been there just waiting for the right time to come out!

Leave those people out your business and away from you!

Why do you need those type of people for? Cause they damn sure aren't your friends!

People are jealous and want your life and your personality! I'm not being around anyone that may feel they have to compete with me! Bye Felicia!

Give me confident sincere people.

Grind, Grind

Truth IS

TRUTH IS...
WHEN I WAS a teen I was insecure. Oh but you can't tell me nothing now!

I wanted a pair of Nike Cleeks so bad but my mom couldn't afford them. Now I can't even shut my closet door because it is full of shoes. The same store I grew up on I am now signed with them!

I was molested didn't think I would ever love a man or for that matter couldn't imagine a man being deeply in love with me. But I'm 17 years in with my best friend! I'm married y'all! We love each other, anyone who knows us knows that. God always said that I would be married. I remember going to work not knowing how the boss would treat me that day! But I never gave up!

Now I'm the boss calling all the shots! I treat my people like people not animals. I remember being talked about wondering how I was going to bounce back from that jab! Now there isn't a place I could go to without someone asking for a picture because I inspire them – they love me.

We have been getting evicted since I was little so I know the struggle all too well.

Now I'm paying my bills months in advance! (y'all need to feel this feeling!)

I say that to say this...

DREAMS DO COME TRUE! WHAT YOU MAY THINK IS YOUR REALITY IS JUST YOUR TEST!! DONT GIVE UP! KEEP THE FAITH. LETS ROCK OUT WITH EACH OTHER. LETS WIN TOGETHER. NOW GET UP!! AND GET YOUR DAY STARTED!

Tonya R

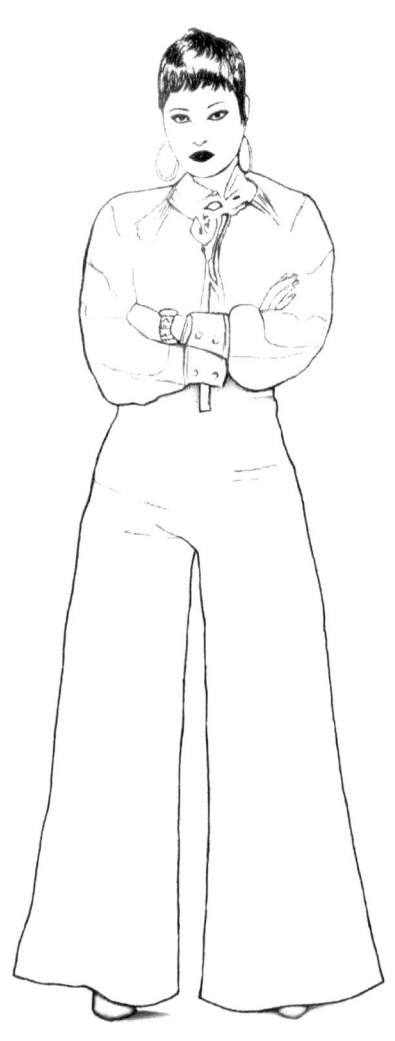

TRUTH IS
Life becomes complicated when you have to depend on a man.

Some of us find ourselves doing the most just to grab attention from them. The things some are willing to do for that man, girls are now doing for free.

That section you are so badly trying to get into doesn't grab his attention in a sexy way, but a thirsty way! That shit holds no value, it gains you no morals, and now you are a joke to those men!

His attention is on the woman over there who brought a table of her own. He's going to respect the woman that respects herself!

Your worries should never be if he has money or not because it will never be yours.

Everything could easily be taken away, like your self-respect. Hold on to that!

Work

TRUTH IS

IMAGINE YOU HAVING an Eviction Notice. On an eviction notice they give you the day and time which you have to move. Now you are trying to scrape together cash. Your focus isn't on anything but that deadline. You have to get so creative you even set your pride to the side and speak up! All you are worrying about is not getting evicted!

IF YOU PUT THAT SAME KIND OF ENERGY EVERYDAY INTO YOUR GOALS DO YOU KNOW HOW SUCCESSFUL YOU WOULD BE? GOOD GOD!

Don't wait till your back is up against the wall to go hard for what you believe in! Go hard now! Trust me, it works.

TRUTH IS...

Life is your choice! Always remember it's what you make it! Make something out of it!

- I didn't graduate from high school when I was supposed to.
- I was a single parent in my teens
- Grew up in Pagedale
- My granny and mom didn't have money to fund our dreams our goals
- I was broken inside from an abusive relationship, shady friends, and molestation

I know what's it like to lose, I've lost before! Houses, cars, my dad, my business you name it!

BUT YET I STILL REFUSE TO GIVE UP!

I didn't think twice to let any of those things make me bitter! I honestly earned everything I have in an honest way. No shady come ups. I didn't get it back then but I get it now. God prepared me for all of this I say this in the most humbled way.

Your life isn't for anyone else to understand.

God don't bless no mess.

If You're Not Ready To Be Talked About, You're Not Ready For Success

TRUTH IS...

THIS IS ONE of the reasons you won't get far in life! Understand one thing about what a person feels or thinks about you or the decisions you make in life is none of your fucking business. You will never get far in life if you care what a person think or who don't like you! Do you know how many people don't like me? Who never met or had one conversation with me?

Man I don't give a damn about any of that! That isn't my business. People don't even know how to approach me in a negative way! So they won't say shit. They just stare real hard as if I don't belong. I found that to be the anointed around me. And that's not me being cocky that's just me knowing the favor I have over my life! Which I believe came from so much praying. I fail where God had to say to himself "let me take a closer look at her"

People are quick to ignore your struggles but real fast to tell you humble yourself when you are celebrating your blessings!

People hate what they don't understand!

I don't give a FUCK who doesn't like you or the way you go hard out of this bitch for yourself! Just always carry yourself in such a way that when they see you they respect you! Understand the world we live in. People will either hate or pay homage! Man y'all have to start thanking God for the people who show their hand early on so you know who to fuck with when shit starts getting real for you!

Cause once you're hot, everyone starts to come around! And you'll end up never knowing the truth!

You have to start digging real deep down in your soul and find that inner strength within you to kill shit. If you want real success you have to know how to handle all that comes with it!

TRUTH IS
Sometimes you got to place yourself in the most uncomfortable situations cause if you want it bad enough you will work hard to keep it!

We all know working hard gives you more. I have seen stylists quit because they afraid they might not make booth rent in time! Forgetting all about the talents God has blessed them with.

I've seen people not purchase that house or buy that car cause they were afraid they wouldn't be able to pay the bill. I've seen the smartest people fail just because they were afraid they might not win.

The law of attraction, in a nutshell, says what you think about, you bring about! SO FEAR NOTHING! I am so fearless it's scary!

TRUTH IS…
Often times things don't happen for us ask quickly or at all as we would like them to because we don't have the resources or the information that we need to get us there or to get us started. And not because it isn't there but we allow our pride to get in the way! Just by simply stepping up or just saying "hey I need help with this" or "I could use that class" or information from that person or persons can sometimes be all you need. In order to go far in life, you need resources, contacts, and information that could possibly help you for a brighter future.

Copy The Right Cat

OPRAH & BILL GATES

TRUTH IS...
I DON'T STRIVE to be like them. But to think like them. That alone has made me very successful in life.

Being successful not only means wealth to me, but also doing what we are known not to do. Things such as, supporting each other, running a successful business without bashing your competitors, teaching without fear that the ones you teach will pass you in life, giving, investing with your race, putting more money in your community, and things like that.

My mission is bigger than what the eyes can see. I have no desire to do anything other than what I've planned to. And I will not allow anything to get in the way of that.

We could be known for so much more. Only if we stick together!

Motives

TRUTH IS...
It's EASIER TO admit when you're wrong instead of being defensive.

Sometimes it's not what you say but how you say it.

Don't let one situation or two steal your joy because no matter how hard a person tries to assassinate your character, real people with an unselfish heart are the ones who genuinely knows understand.

It could be really hard being in the public eye because some peoples job and agendas are to stand in front of the public just to TRY and hurt you.

But it's a secret that most of us live by and that's no matter what find the good in it all. So even when someone is being super extra, there's something beautiful laying deep in that situation. Negative vibes taught me how to be positive and I'm thankful for that!

You Inspire Me

TRUTH IS...
LET MY HUSTLE inspire you in a positive way.

Most of us are judging others from what another person has said about them. As woman we could be a little insecure than men so because of that we wish to not like that person anyway. It could be because of their hustle, the way they look, or the way they dress etc. We already want to believe they aren't as perfect as the selfies they take. So we tend to run with the information we heard about them. Not thinking for one second just maybe the person who's telling the story may need a little empowerment herself because of the insecurities within her. It takes some kind of woman to destroy the next, but here is where it ends! I will never down the next woman I am not cancer I will not try to destroy the human body with the words that come out my mouth. What I will do is breathe life into her.

But Darling, What If You Fly?

TRUTH IS...

SOME OF US are so afraid of the unknown, that we bury our minds with the 'what if's'. That easily turns into discouragement. So the first thing we do is turn to what's more comfortable for us. Not knowing, sometimes, it takes for us to place ourselves in uncomfortable situations, those situations soon turns into the best things ever!

Example:

You have talent, you may have what it takes to become successful, a millionaire, a mogul! But, again, the fear of the unknown turns into the what ifs that easily turns into discouragement. So you stick at that shitty job you hate but it's an easy paycheck. Just watch others live out the same dreams you want for yourself.

Most of us successful people are always uncomfortable but we are believers, we are risk-takers, and therefore we are successful. You are stopping yourself! Nothing is easy. It is not easy to become successful! So stop allowing the unknown to control you! Go get uncomfortable.

Don't Get Mad, Get Motivated

TRUTH IS...
SOMETIMES WE GET so upset and mad from the actions of others that we tend to breakdown. Heartbreak, He said she said, drama, breakup, loss of a job, and just negativity all around.

All these things are to push you even harder! This is your chance to show out! This is your chance to prove to yourself that you are much stronger than you think! You are worthy and capable of overcoming all the BS that's weighing down on you!

DONT GET MAD GO HARD!
Start planning your come up! Don't speak on it (start planning)! Let them inspire you! get motivated from the BS that's thrown your way!

Go SO HARD that you shock yourself!

Sometimes we have to learn from all the hate, the negativity, the bashings, and the beatings. Go over your issues and find the solutions.

For example:

Okay I'm not shit - well let me work on that. My house is dirty - okay let me clean it up.
My credit bad- okay let me fix it.
My kids don't listen - okay let me put my foot down.
I'm broke - okay time to get money.
Sometimes you have to take the bad with the good!
Sometimes you have to start thanking those who shine a light on you.
Sometimes it may take a person exposing your flaws your weakness your battles for you to wake up and get it right.

So don't GET MAD, GET MOTIVATED!
I haven't seen a person who talks crap about doing better than me yet. So don't let the words, the hate, and the hurt from others define you!

What's A Hater?

TRUTH IS...
HATERS DON'T HATE you,

Some just hate the situations they are in and it is very hard for them to be happy about your situation.

They picture themselves with the life you have and some go as far as mimicking everything that you do.

Some don't even really want your life; they want to be able to show you

"whatever you can do I can do better"

And mess it up every time because that's not what God is calling them to do.

Haters don't hate you they hate the situation that you are, some may feel they deserve more than you, these kind of people like to think you're not being blessed it's the devil who's giving you them things. This is because deep down inside they feel they are better than you.

Remember what I said up there "anything you can do I can do better"? Yeah. They like to think that! So because they think they are better, your blessings aren't blessings, and because they feel that in a way they could never give you a blessing (that's why haters don't congratulate). These kind of people like to turn their guilt on you, they will go so far to try and destroy you that they are destroying their character. Because they think everyone can see the hating that they are doing towards you they assassinate your character!

That's when the hating begins!

There will be fake pages about you, gossiping about you to just about anyone who will listen etc. But catch this, some may be nice!

Watch out for them kind they hate you so much it turns into an effectuation! That's the most dangerous kind! See they want you to be shocked about the things they do they want you to hurt! So they do they shit in small pieces. That kind of hate linger on for years!

Listen to your gut! Get rid of all them kind of people. It's like a cancer if you don't get rid of it it's going to spread all through your life.

Don't Do It For Social Media

TRUTH IS…
THE SAME WAY we are going to send our kids to school on the first day well dressed, nice hairdos and haircuts, backpacks filled with school supplies are the same way we should send them all year around! We are full time parents not part time OUR CHILDREN REPRESENT US! What we teach our kids affect them in the long run!

If we teach to never put extra time in their hygiene, making sure they are well dressed, making sure their beds and rooms are cleaned before leaving the house will only lead to them growing up will bad habits! I love seeing all the back to school photos but it saddens me knowing it only last for that first week!

These teachers are getting younger and THEY TALK! SO PLEASE DONT LEAVE THEM NO CHOICE BUT TO TALK ABOUT YOUR CHILDREN! Let's do better! Set some good examples for our baby's they only learn what they see and if you don't care they won't.

Imagine How Hard It Is For You To Change

Tonya R

TRUTH IS...
WOMEN ALWAYS THINK they are going to be the one who change their partner. Absolutely not!

Karma is real, know that!

So don't be mad, sad, or hurt trust me shit isn't going to work out! And if you have someone that truly loves you don't go messing up what you have for these bums! Terrible parents, trifling, miserable, liar's, broke as a damn joke, their whole situation is fucked up. That's why they go so hard to try to fuck your shit up!

Grass may seem greener on the other side. But man, STAY WHERE YALL AT!

You Didn't Work This Hard To Stay Just The Same

TRUTH IS ...

Every day, I'm praying and working as hard as possible for things NOT to remain the same. So many individuals have come at me saying "you've changed" I'm doing everything in my power to change my ways to what is pleasing to God. My way failed me, too many times. God has been slapping me in the face with blessings, a renewed spirit, and happy life ever since I put him first and allowed Christ to rise up and grow in me.

Some people I grew apart from, because they didn't want to grow. I refused to be held down and now I'm here to please God. Not hold on to any relationship in the flesh that would hinder the only important relationship my life depends on. Don't stop growing!

Emotional Thinking Is Stinking Thinking

TRUTH IS...
IN BUSINESS YOU have to be able to look a person in the eyes and tell them the truth. Hold your head up and be firm because communication is everything! In business you have to be able to listen and you have to be able to talk to people.

In business there is nothing worse than a person who needs somebody but can't shut up and listen. You don't know everything! And there's nothing wrong with taking notes.

In business you have leave your feelings at the door! The sign of weakness is a sign of failure. No one wants a weak individual on their team and no one wants to be affiliated with a weak person in business.

Another thing! It's all in who you know in business your contacts in your cellphone should be mean!

You should be able to pick up your phone and have a resource for whatever it is that you need! That's called building business relationships! In business, you build bridges. PLEASE DON'T BURN THEM.

In business you have to understand everyone that starts with you isn't going to finish with you. You have to be okay with that.

Leaders do not create followers they create more leaders. Either they were inspired by you to move on or just simply wanting and believing in themselves. As a boss and a leader you must be okay with the decisions of others. You have to wish them well (and mean it). Then, MOVE ON!

There is always room for new people who want to be in that same position they once were in to learn and get inspired to want more out of life. And you have to welcome them with open arms just like you did the others.

Truth IS

Some of my greatest friends, my best coworkers, have moved on and till this day we love and root for each other cause that's what secure sincere leaders do. In life you have to believe in yourself even if it's the most uncomfortable thing.

And never ever take anything in business personal.

Stick To Your Thing,

TRUTH IS...

EMPOWERING IS MY thing. So everything in business that I do will be based around that. Don't go all crazy doing what others are doing just because it works for them. Find your truth and stick with that. Whatever you are good at start there. Warren buffet taught me that success is for anyone who truly wants it.

Write the vision and make it plain. What's your thing?

_____
_____
_____
_____
_____
_____
_____
_____
_____
_____
_____
_____
_____
_____
_____
_____
_____
_____
_____
_____
_____.

Someday Is Not A Day On The Calendar

Truth IS

TODAY, I'M WORKING on a big project that I simply would have kept putting off if I had not set the date and hired the help. You MUST set the date.

TRUTH IS…
There's just something about going to sleep with a clear conscience. So, before you go to sleep, vent to God. Give Him your care, your rough day, the bills, the troubled relationships, your frustrations, and whatever else. Rest in the fact that HE holds the UNIVERSE in the palm of His hands. He can take care of your stresses much better than you can.

TRUTH IS…
I'd rather show off the people's lives I've been able to change for the better instead showing off every single thing that I'm able to buy. You can tell who doesn't really have it because they go above and beyond to convince everyone that they do. Show me how you are helping others do better in their finances, lives, and business. Now that's impressive.

In The Face Of Adversity, Which One Of These Are You?

1. **Cop-outs**: These people set no goals and make no decisions.
2. **Hold-outs**: These people have beautiful dreams, but they are afraid to respond to challenges because they lack the self-confidence to overcome difficulties.
3. **Drop-outs**: These individuals clearly define their goals, and, in the beginning, they work hard to make their dreams come true. However, when the going gets tough, they quit.
4. **All-outs**: These are the stars. They want to shine as an inspiration to others. Once all-outs have set their goals, they never quit. Even when the price gets high and the challenges mount, they're dedicated. Their 'cando' attitude carries them to greatness.

Domestic Tips

Truth IS

For me, Sunday's are for cleaning the spirit and your house. Keep up with your domestic duties by setting text alerts! Every month I clean the fridge with 1/4 cup of white vinegar, 1 tbs baking soda, a few drops of lavender essential oil and one cup of warm water. BOOM nice clean fresh fridge.

25 Uses For Epsom Salt

1. **Lawn and garden** — Studies show that the magnesium and sulfur that comprise Epsom salt may help your plants grow greener, produce higher yields and have more blooms!
2. **Pedicure** — Combine 1/2 cup Epsom salt and warm soapy water, then soak your feet for 5 minutes to soften skin. Remove nail polish, push back cuticles, then cut and file your nails. Soak an additional 5 minutes in a warm Epsom bath for super soft feet.
3. **Hair volumizer** — Combine equal parts conditioner and Epsom salt. Work the mixture through your hair and leave for 20 minutes. The result? Hair full of va-va-voom and volume!
4. **Facial scrub** — This is one of my favorite Epsom salt uses. Mix 1/2 tsp of Epsom salt with your favorite cleanser; massage into skin using small circles to give your pores a deep-cleaning. Rinse your face with cool water, pat dry. This is one of the most refreshing Epsom salt uses!
5. **Relax** — Add two cups of Epsom salt to your very-warm bath water and soak for 15 minutes. You can purchase Epsom salt with lavender or eucalyptus for an extra-soothing bath experience. Be careful when standing up, you'll find that you are VERY relaxed after your Epsom salt bath.
6. **Sea salt texturizing hair spray** — Combine 1 cup of hot water, 2 tablespoons Epsom salt, 1 teaspoon aloe Vera gel and 1/2 tsp conditioner in a spray bottle. Spray salt mixture into hair and scrunch hair with your hand for pretty beachy-waves.
7. **Fabric softener crystals** — Mix 4 cups of Epsom salt and 20 drops of essential oil to make DIY fabric softener crystals. Use 1/4 cup per load and add at beginning of wash. What a clever way to use Epsom salt, and also a way to save money!
8. **Splinter removal** — Soak your finger in an Epsom salt bath for easy splinter extraction.
9. **Body scrub** — After showering, massage handfuls of Epsom salt over wet skin to exfoliate the body. Get a spa treatment at home! Get more facial scrub recipes here.

10. **Exfoliation** — For exfoliation, mix 2 cups of Epsom salt with 1/4 cup of petroleum jelly and a few drops of lavender essential oil. Gently massage into dry patches for smoother skin.
11. **Mosquito bites** — Epsom salt can ease the symptoms of mosquito bites. Make a compress by soaking a washcloth in cold water that has been mixed with Epsom salt (2 tablespoons per cup of water), then gently apply to the bite area. This is yet another one of my favorite Epsom salt uses.
12. **Sore muscles and arthritis** — If your muscles or joints ache, an Epsom salt bath is a great way to find relief. Add 2 cups of Epsom salt to your very-warm bath water, agitate the water with your hands to dissolve it then soak for 15 minutes.
13. **Tile cleaner** — Mix equal parts of dish soap and Epsom salt for a super easy and effective tile cleaner. Rinse with clear water. This is one of the most frugal Epsom salt uses, a great way to save on cleaning supplies and to use a natural alternative to harsh chemical cleaners!
14. **Bedtime bath for kids** — Add one cup of Epsom salt to your kids' evening bath to help them sleep more peacefully.
15. **Headache relief** — Evidence shows that that soaking in an Epsom salt bath can relieve headache symptoms.
16. **Acne** — Epsom salt has antibacterial, antifungal and antiviral properties making it a fantastic natural treatment for acne.
17. **Remove odor on hands and feet** — Add 3 Tablespoons of Epsom salt to 1 quart of warm water and soak your hands or feet for 15 minutes. This will make your skin soft, your nails shine, and also help remove foul odors.
18. **Relieve constipation** — Pour 8 oz. of drinking water into a glass, mix with 1 to 2 tsp. of Epsom salt and drink the mixture for immediate relief of constipation. Mixing directions are also found on most Epsom salt packages, consult your physician before trying this.
19. **Sunburn relief** — Dissolve two tablespoons of Epsom salt in 1 cups of water and spray on minor sunburns.

20. **Draw out infection** — For simple infections on hands or feet, soak in a hot Epsom salt bath for 10 minutes to help clear the area. Note, some staph infections are worsened by soaking in hot water, consult your physician.
21. **Cure for common cold** — Did you know that Epsom salt baths can speed healing by detoxifying your body and increasing your white blood cell count? Try an Epsom salt bath the next time you feel those first symptoms of a cold.
22. **Reduce swelling** — Epsom salt baths can help the appearance of bruises and reduce swelling.
23. **Deter slugs** — Sprinkle a trail of Epsom salt around the area you want to be free of slugs.
24. **Blackhead removal** — Mix a teaspoon of Epsom salt, 3 drops iodine and half a cup of boiling water. Dab this solution to your blackheads with a cotton ball to help naturally extract them.
25. **Insecticide** — Mix Epson salt with water, add to a spray bottle and spray on plants to naturally deter insects.

By: Adriana Caho

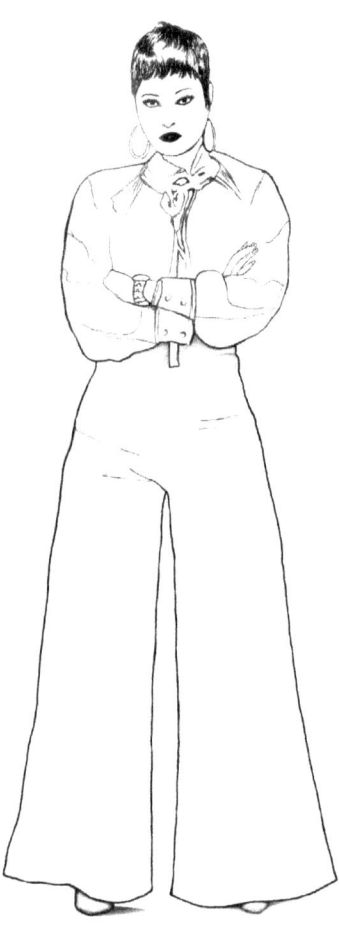

"I don'1 allow others or myself to say, "it's always something." I don'1 because the connotation is that there's always something bad right around the corner. And I know that the God I serve has blessed me far too much to speak of the grace He's given and the mercy He's shown me in such a way. That's blasphemy so; watch your words because they rule your life. Be thankful even when it's tough because I'm a living witness that His grace is sufficient"

My Famous Recipes

Tonya R

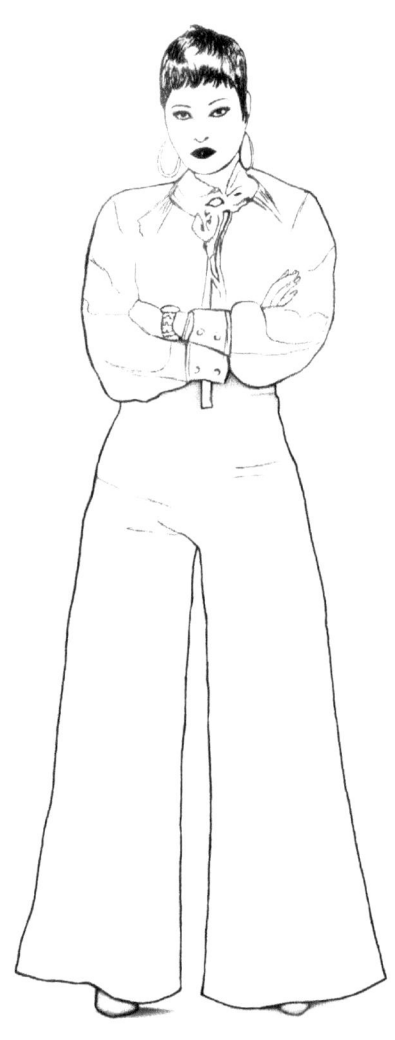

Famous Mac And Cheese

YOU WILL NEED:

- VELVEEDA CHEESE BRICK
- MACARONI NOODLES
- PEPPER
- FLOUR
- MILK
- HOT SAUCE
- PRE HEAT OVEN TO 350

Boil noodles, cut cheese brick into cubes, and melt in non-stick pot on low (while stirring), add 2-3 cups of milk to cheese while melting, add few drops of hot sauce and pepper to cheese sauce.

In a separate pan melt one stick of butter and 1 tablespoon of flour together and stir.

After cheese melted, add noodles to pan, add cheese to noodles and butter and flour and stir until all mixed TOGETHER GOOD….

Throw in oven and bake until browned on top. DONE!

BEST MAC AND CHEESE IN THE WORLD!!!

Sweet Potatos

YOU WILL NEED:

4-5 SWEET POTATOS
1 STICK OF BUTTER
CINNAMON
SUGAR

CUT POTATOES INTO SLICES, ADD ONE STICK OF BUTTER, 1 CUP OF SUGAR, ADD CINNAMON, AND ADD WATER TO COVER TOP OF POTATOS.

BRING TO A BOIL THEN TURN DOWN TO SIMMER AND COVER.

ADD SUGAR AS IT COOKS. THE SYRUPY THE BETTER.

COOK UNTIL POTATOES ARE TENDER. DONE!

BEST POTATOS IN THE WORLD!

Collard Greens

YOU WILL NEED:

2-3 BAGS OF COLLARD GREENS
1 HEAD OF CABBAGE
TURKEY NECK
4-5 LARGE CANS OF CHICKEN BROTH (ANY BRAND)

BRING A COUPLE CANS OF BROTH TO A BOIL, ADD TURKEY NECKS AND COOK UNTIL DONE.

ADD GREENS AND COOK ON MEDIUM HEAT FOR ABOUT 25 MINUTES OR SO, ADD MORE BROTH AS NEEDED, TURN TO SIMMER

AND COVER. ONCE GREENS ALMOST DONE, CHOP UP CABBAGE

AND ADD CABBAGE TO POT AND COOK FOR ANOTHER 10-15 MINUTES. SEASON TO TASTE AND COOK TO TENDERNESS DESIRED. DONE!

BEST COLLARD GREENS IN THE WORLD!

Dear Reader,
Thank you for your purchase. I truly appreciate you taking the time out of your life to read my book. Your input is important to me. Please don't forget to write a review and be honest.

God bless,
Tonya Rush

Truth IS

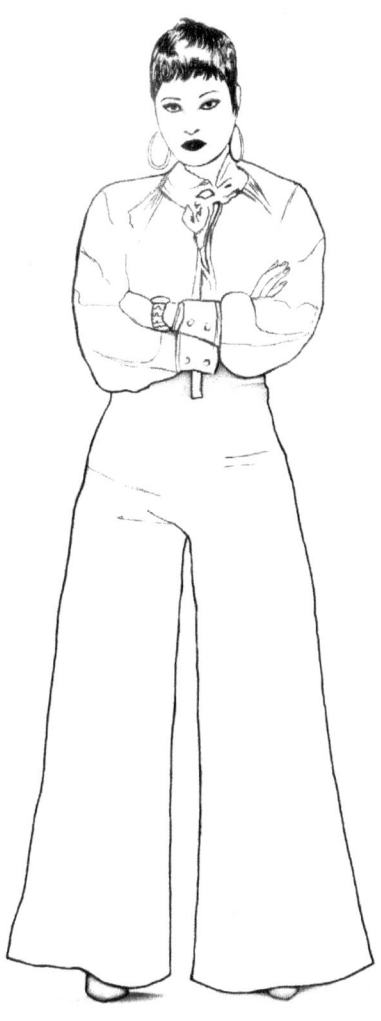

All this truth simply to say There's almost nothing that I can look back on and not be able to say, "that's why that happened." The cliché, "everything happens for a reason" is a hard pill to swallow when you're in the midst of your storm. Your setback, your betrayal or even your heartache.

You're clouded during the moment and you can't see straight. Just hold on! Time has an interesting way of revealing things that allow you to understand the what, when, why and whatever else you need to get your full understanding. This, Love-bugs is where your faith kicks in and will even be tested. Yon can't just use the sayings and the clichés when it's convenient. Faith allows you to walk in a way the grace carries you through it all even when you can't see a light at the end of the tunnel.

My life has shown me that I no longer need to see the light. I just need to move. The light will come. Nothing last forever. Not even the best of things so, there's no way that a storm would either.

The wrap up here is this…I don't allow others or myself to say, "it's always something." I don't because the connotation is that there's always something bad right around the corner. And I know that the God I serve has blessed me far too much to speak of the grace He's given and the mercy He's shown me in such a way. That's blasphemy so; watch your words because they rule your life. Be thankful even when that His grace is it's tough because I'm a living witness!!

About the Author

With beauty and poise, multi-talented Author, Speaker, Inspirer and Entrepreneur Tonya Rush influence women and men to stand in their truth and evolve in their business and personal life. She enjoys presenting inspirational conversations on the importance of being an extraordinary woman and man. With her witty personality, her ability to emphasize and candid truth, she will pour into you her experiences, failures, successes and challenges that she had to face and overcome in order to evolve into a woman of influence that can confidently and proudly say "I'm standing in my truth"...she understands what self-accountability means and she believes that once you "own your truths" and change your mindset to begin to live the life you deserve.

Her mantra is "Although truth hurts, truth also heals".

She uses her 20 plus years as a serial entrepreneur/business woman and 5 years as and certified life coach to create a platform that allow her to influence, impact, and ignite others to change their mindset to change their life by learning how to accentuate personal responsibility and stand in their truth spiritually, mentally and physically.

She obtained her life coaching certification through Tony Gaskins Life Coaching School. She is also the Author of an urban fiction Amazon bestselling book titled Grimey Enough. Quickly she realized that she had a passion and a God given calling to inspire the masses with her reality based thought process, savvy business motivation and positive words and advice, she changed genres to self-help and her new book is titled "Truth Is" that proves that although sometimes truth hurts, is also heals. She jumps out the bed every morning and hit the floor thanking God because she knows she will be the reason that a mindset will shift and they will not only believe but will become. For Tonya, this is bigger than empowering, she's on a mission to change the mindset of every woman and man whose been counted out and broken.

She expanded her platform to young adults ages 13-29 because Tonya understands that broken children grow up to be broken adults.

Tonya resides in St. Louis Missouri with her husband of 17 years and two children ages 14 and 22. She is a philanthropist and the founder of a nonprofit organization called "A-lot-of-socks" and our mission is to donate socks to the homeless and underprivileged men, women, children, and seniors. When Tonya not working as the CEO of a successful home health care agency, she enjoys writing, coaching, cooking, traveling, going to church and spending time with her family.

The most important accomplishments in her life, according to Tonya, is being a wife and mother. Everything else is just a bonus.

Xo,

Tonya R

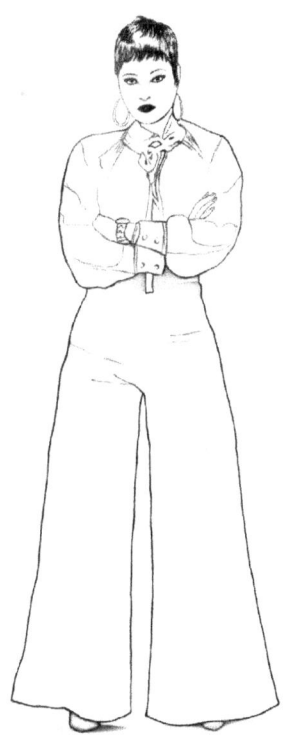

Tonya's website is www.tonyarush.com

STAY CONNECTED TO ME

Follow me on Twitter @AuthorTonyaj
Follow me on Facebook @Tonya Rush
"LIKE" my page on Facebook @Author Tonya Rush

Follow me on Instagram @tonyarushdotcom

Follow me on snap chat @tonyainspires

Visit my website WWW.TONYARUSH.COM

www.ingramcontent.com/pod-product-compliance
Lightning Source LLC
Chambersburg PA
CBHW051120160426
43195CB00014B/2270